PRACTICE TESTS

Amy Bohmann
Texas Lutheran University

SOCIAL PSYCHOLOGY

TWELFTH EDITION

Shelley E. Taylor
University of California, Los Angeles

Letitia Anne Peplau
University of California, Los Angeles

David O. Sears
University of California, Los Angeles

PEARSON
Prentice Hall

Upper Saddle River, New Jersey 07458

PEARSON
Prentice Hall

© 2006 by PEARSON EDUCATION, INC.
Upper Saddle River, New Jersey 07458

All rights reserved

10 9 8 7 6 5 4 3 2 1

ISBN 0-13-193282-9

Printed in the United States of America

Table of Contents

Practice Problems:

Chapter 1:	Theories and Methods in Social Psychology	1
Chapter 2:	Person Perception	7
Chapter 3:	Social Cognition	13
Chapter 4:	The Self	19
Chapter 5:	Attitudes and Attitude Change	25
Chapter 6:	Prejudice	31
Chapter 7:	Social Influence	37
Chapter 8:	Interpersonal Attraction	42
Chapter 9:	Close Relationships	47
Chapter 10:	Behavior in Groups	53
Chapter 11:	Gender	59
Chapter 12:	Helping Behavior	65
Chapter 13:	Aggression	71
Chapter 14:	Social Psychology and Health	76
Chapter 15:	Social Psychology and the Law	81

Answers to Exercises:

Chapter 1:	Theories and Methods in Social Psychology	86
Chapter 2:	Person Perception	88
Chapter 3:	Social Cognition	90
Chapter 4:	The Self	93
Chapter 5:	Attitudes and Attitude Change	95
Chapter 6:	Prejudice	97
Chapter 7:	Social Influence	100
Chapter 8:	Interpersonal Attraction	102
Chapter 9:	Close Relationships	104
Chapter 10:	Behavior in Groups	107
Chapter 11:	Gender	110
Chapter 12:	Helping Behavior	112
Chapter 13:	Aggression	115
Chapter 14:	Social Psychology and Health	118
Chapter 15:	Social Psychology and the Law	120

Chapter 1: Theories and Methods in Social Psychology

Multiple Choice

Circle the letter beside the response that best answers the question or completes the statement.

1. The level of analysis used by clinical and personality psychologists is:

    a. individual
    b. societal
    c. interpersonal
    d. macro-level

2. The tendency to lash out when people are blocked from achieving a desired goal is explained by:

    a. individualism
    b. Gestalt psychology
    c. expectancy-value theory
    d. the frustration-aggression hypothesis

3. Which influential theory suggests that people perceive situations or events not as made up of many discrete elements but rather as "dynamic wholes"?

    a. psychoanalytic
    b. behaviorism
    c. learning
    d. Gestalt

4. A person's desire to join clubs and go to social events while attempting to establish a sense of belonging in college is best explained by which general theory in social psychology?

    a. learning theory
    b. motivational theory
    c. cognitive theory
    d. decision-making theory

5. According to cognitive theories, why do cheerleaders grab our attention at football games when there are 50,000 other people present?

   a. Proximity: They are closer to us than some of the others in the stadium, so we tend to notice them first.
   b. Similarity: They are often our peers, and we pay attention because we share similarities with them.
   c. Figure/ground: They stand out as figures against the ground because they yell and wear colorful uniforms.
   d. Past experience: They have been associated with football games in the past, so we have become conditioned to seek them out.

6. When the outcomes one person receives depend at least in part on the behavior of the other and vice versa, the people are said to be:

   a. conjoined
   b. independent
   c. dependent
   d. interdependent

7. The term social _____ refers to the set of norms that apply to people in a particular position, such as teacher or student.

   a. status
   b. role
   c. position
   d. action

8. Cultures that emphasize loyalty to the family, adherence to group norms, and the preservation of harmony in social relations with members of one's own group are described as:

   a. individualist
   b. communalities
   c. collectivist
   d. acculturated

9. Adaptive responses to specific problems that were encountered by our ancestors are:

   a. inherited traits
   b. evolved psychological mechanisms
   c. genetically-based traits
   d. evolved traits

10. Social psychologists frequently develop theories that focus on a limited range of phenomena. What are these theories called?

    a. minimalist theories
    b. middle-range theories
    c. focused theories
    d. none of the above

11. Which of the following is not one of the goals of social psychological research?

    a. description
    b. causal analysis
    c. application
    d. all of these are goals of research

12. A _____ sample means that each person in the larger population to which we wish to generalize has an equal chance of being included in the study.

    a. quota
    b. systematic
    c. cross-cultural
    d. random

13. Undergraduate students are used in 75% of published articles in social psychology because:

    a. They are convenient for university researchers to use.
    b. They generalize to the population better than any other group.
    c. They will do most anything the researcher asks.
    d. They represent "ideal" participants.

14. A researcher is interested in the effects of rejection on self-esteem. Participants are brought into the laboratory and led to believe that other participants have either accepted them or rejected them. Their self-esteem is then measured. In this study, rejection is the:

    a. dependent variable
    b. independent variable
    c. measured variable
    d. none of the above

15. Which of the following can be conducted in both the laboratory and the field?

    a. experimental research
    b. correlational research
    c. both (a) and (b)
    d. neither type of research can be conducted in both settings

16. The fact that the results of an experiment are more likely to be valid in situations outside the specific research situation itself is known as:

   a. internal validity
   b. external validity
   c. reliability
   d. general reliability

17. Which of the following is an acceptable solution to the research problem of experimenter bias?

   a. a "blind" technique
   b. extreme standardization of the research setting
   c. both (a) and (b)
   d. none of the above

18. As part of an introductory psychology class, Kevin is required to participate in experiments. Because he thinks that the requirement is ridiculous, Kevin tries to sabotage each experiment in which he participates. According to Weber and Cook, Kevin would be described as a (an):

   a. good subject
   b. negativistic subject
   c. apprehensive subject
   d. faithful subject

19. The use of different research procedures to explore the same conceptual relationship is a (an):

   a. exact replication
   b. operational definition
   c. conceptual replication
   d. repeat methodology

20. The committee of researchers at universities and research institutions that is responsible for ensuring that all research is conducted according to a set of general principles laid down by the federal government is the:

   a. Research Regulatory Committee
   b. Institutional Research Committee
   c. University Research Association
   d. Institutional Review Board

True-False

Place the letter "T" beside each statement that is true, and place the letter "F" beside each statement that is totally or partially false.

1. The individual level of analysis is typically used by clinical and personality psychologists.

2. Social psychologists emphasize the power of the situation because change in the social context often elicits change in the individual.

3. Behaviorists typically focus on covert behavior.

4. The core idea of social exchange theory is that as two people interact with each other, they exchange benefits and costs.

5. Demographers predict that, in the United States, the proportions of European Americans will increase and the proportion of Asian Americans will decrease over this century.

6. Social values are rules and expectations about how group members should behave.

7. The greatest strength of the experimental method is that it avoids the ambiguities about causality that characterize correlational studies.

8. Internal validity is high when results of a study can be generalized beyond the immediate research setting.

9. Field research is typically higher in internal validity than laboratory research.

10. "Minimal risk" for research participants means that the risks anticipated in the research are no greater "than those ordinarily encountered in daily life."

Fill-in-the-Blank

1. _____ is a historical approach that influenced social psychology. It emphasizes the measurement of observable behavior.

2. Cultures that value personal independence and self-reliance are said to be high in _____.

3. _____ applies the principles of natural selection to the understanding of human behavior and social life.

4. _____ help psychologists to organize what they know about social behavior and suggest new predictions that can be tested in further research.

5. The _____ problem occurs when two variables are related to each other, but either could plausibly be the causal agent.

6. The possibility that some unmeasured, unforeseen, or unspecified factor might influence the correlation observed between two variables is known as the _____ problem in correlational research.

7. When conducting experimental research, _____ of participants to conditions is crucial to be sure there are no preexisting differences between the groups being compared.

8. When researchers are confident that the effects observed in the dependent variable are the result of the independent variable, an experiment is said to be high in _____.

9. _____ relies on data that were originally collected for some other purpose.

10. An advantage of _____ is that when participants complete a survey or research task, their data is already recorded for the researcher.

Chapter 2: Person Perception

Multiple Choice

Circle the letter beside the response that best answers the question or completes the statement.

1. Salient stimuli:

    a. produce the most extreme evaluative judgments
    b. are seen as the most causally powerful
    c. produce more consistency of judgment
    d. all of the above

2. The idea that certain traits seem to go along together is known as:

    a. the halo effect
    b. implicit personality theory
    c. the assimilation effect
    d. the contrast effect

3. The distinction between category-based impressions and more individuated impressions is called _____.

    a. categorization
    b. schematic processing
    c. dual processing
    d. assimilation

4. When individuals are processing information about another person at a relatively superficial or stereotypic level, _____ is more likely.

    a. contrast
    b. assimilation
    c. categorization
    d. dual processing

5. According to the assimilation effect, being interviewed for a job simultaneously with a highly competent other should have what effect on the interviewer's perception of your competence level?

    a. It should increase the interviewer's perception of your competence.
    b. It should decrease the interviewer's perception of your competence.
    c. It should have no effect on the interviewer's perception of your competence.
    d. It should set up a competition between you and the other interviewee.

6. Stephanie is going out on a blind date with Michael. Based on reports of people who know Michael, Stephanie has heard that Michael is funny, sincere, athletic, egocentric, and unpredictable. According to the negativity effect and Anderson's weighted averaging model, which of the following traits will Stephanie weigh more heavily in forming her impression of Michael?

    a. sincere
    b. athletic
    c. egocentric
    d. funny

7. An abstract ideal of a schema is called a (an):

    a. exemplar
    b. stereotype
    c. prototype
    d. model

8. In which situation are we least motivated to make an accurate decision, and therefore may use rapid, heuristically-based information processing rather than careful, systematic processing?

    a. deciding which surgeon should perform a risky surgery on us
    b. deciding which classmate should be our lab partner, as this may affect our grade in the course
    c. deciding which cashier should check us out at the grocery store
    d. deciding which person we should hire for an important project

9. You are sitting in your 10 AM class, and you are very preoccupied because you have an exam in your next class at 11:00. Your 10:00 professor is handing back homework assignments and gives you one that doesn't belong to you. Considering your emotional state, how would you most likely explain her behavior?

    a. She doesn't care about students much; after all, she doesn't even know my name.
    b. She must be so rushed for time that she didn't have a chance to get a good look at the name on the page.
    c. She was preoccupied today and thought she read my name on that page by mistake.
    d. It's early in the semester and therefore so easy to confuse students' names.

10. According to Jones and Davis, all of the following are useful cues in making dispositional (internal) attributions except:

    a. choice
    b. social role
    c. consensus
    d. social desirability

11. The fact that people try to see if a particular effect and a particular cause go together across different situations is known as _____.

    a. prototypes
    b. covariation
    c. dual processing
    d. simultaneous processing

12. According to Kelley's theory, which of the following is NOT a type of information used in arriving at causal attributions?

    a. social desirability
    b. distinctiveness
    c. consensus
    d. consistency

13. The tendency for actors to infer situational causes for their own behavior whereas observers tend to infer dispositional causes for the behavior of others is known as the:

    a. actor-observer effect
    b. salience distortion
    c. "action-focus"
    d. attributional fallacy

14. The tendency to exaggerate how common one's own opinions or behaviors are is called:

    a. the false uniqueness effect
    b. the centrality of the "I"
    c. the "Me" syndrome
    d. the false consensus effect

15. The tendency to underestimate others' standing on attributes that make one distinctive is called:

    a. the false uniqueness effect
    b. the centrality of the "I"
    c. the "Me" syndrome
    d. the false consensus effect

16. When they perform well on a test, students frequently say that they are smart or that they studied hard for the test. On the other hand, when they perform poorly on a test, students alter their attributions, saying that the teacher made the test too challenging or that they were having a bad day. These attributions in response to success and failure reflect the:

    a. actor-observer effect
    b. false consensus effect
    c. self-serving attributional bias
    d. self-centered bias

17. It would be most difficult to distinguish happiness from _____ when judging another person's emotional state.

    a. interest
    b. arousal
    c. attentiveness
    d. surprise

18. Which of the following are included within the visible channel of nonverbal communication?

    a. distance
    b. gesture
    c. eye contact
    d. all of the above

19. Variations in speech are called _____.

    a. visible channels
    b. paralanguage
    c. intonations
    d. expressiveness

20. Biting your lower lip, blinking more than usual, and looking overly nervous while lying are examples of _____.

    a. correspondent inferences
    b. paralanguage
    c. self-serving attributions
    d. nonverbal leakage

True-False

Place the letter "T" beside each statement that is true, and place the letter "F" beside each statement that is totally or partially false.

1. Our knowledge and expectations about others are determined by the impressions we form of them.

2. Overall, people tend to be more positive than negative in their evaluation of others.

3. Contrast refers to a biasing effect on judgments toward the environmental context.

4. People weigh positive information more heavily than negative information in arriving at a complete impression.

5. A major problem with models of impression formation is that people tend to form evaluatively inconsistent characterizations of others.

6. Bad, painful, and unpleasant events inspire a search for causal attributions.

7. We are more likely to make situational attributes for the behavior of people we know very well than for those we know less well.

8. People are as likely to take responsibility for failure as they are for success.

9. People perceive the external, visible attributes of others fairly accurately.

10. Recent research shows that people are generally more accurate judging emotions when those emotions are expressed by members of their own cultural group than when they are expressed by members of a different cultural group.

Fill-in-the-Blank

1. Brightness, noisiness, motion, or novelty are objective conditions that make an object seem more _____.

2. _____ leads us to move from an incident of behavior, to inferring a trait, to inferring other traits, to inferring an entire portrait of a person's personality.

3. Judgments that are biased away from the environmental context show evidence of _____ effects.

4. According to the averaging principle, we make an overall impression by averaging all traits of a person, but putting more weight on those we believe are most _____.

5. We often judge traits (that we don't know about) to be consistent with traits we've already perceived. This is known as _____.

6. We are less likely to attribute a behavior to any particular cause if more than one potential cause is likely. This is called _____.

7. The _____ occurs when we make an internal attribution for successes and an external attribution for failures.

8. We are not particularly accurate in perceiving people, but we are accurate enough to achieve our relationship goals. This type of accuracy is called _____.

9. _____ can provide a rough but reliable measure of interpersonal intimacy.

10. The phenomenon by which people's true emotions "leak out" is _____.

Chapter 3: Social Cognition

Multiple Choice

Circle the letter beside the response that best answers the questions or completes the statement.

1. The study of how people form inferences from the social information in the environment is:

    a. person perception
    b. social cognition
    c. inferential psychology
    d. social information processing

2. Which of the following is a step in the social inference process?

    a. gathering information
    b. deciding what information to use
    c. integrating information into a judgment
    d. all of the above are steps in the social inference process

3. Data about a large number of people are known as:

    a. statistical information
    b. case history information
    c. sampling information
    d. quantified information

4. In drawing inferences about people or events, which type of information is given more weight?

    a. positive information
    b. negative information
    c. positive and negative information are given equal weight
    d. the positivity or negativity of the information has no relationship to social inference

5. Figuring out "what goes with what" in social life is really assessing:

    a. statistical information
    b. case history information
    c. covariation
    d. none of the above

6. Incorrectly perceiving that there are more admissions to hospital emergency rooms on the nights of a full moon would be an example of a (an):

   a. self-fulfilling prophecy
   b. logical error
   c. illusory correlation
   d. representative heuristic

7. Which of the following is a basis for the illusory correlation effect?

   a. associative meaning
   b. paired distinctiveness
   c. both (a) and (b)
   d. none of the above

8. Remembering information that fits the valence of one's current mood state is:

   a. mood consistency
   b. mood-congruent memory
   c. recall similarity
   d. none of the above

9. Jan is in a negative mood, and has to make a decision about whether to take a job that could be very lucrative, but the company is in a bad position, and therefore may fold soon. She can stay risk-free in her current job, but she won't have a chance to make the salary she'd like. Jan has chosen to avert risk. According to Lerner and Keltner, which type of negative mood does Jan most likely possess?

   a. negative—depressed
   b. negative—fearful
   c. negative—angry
   d. negative—sad

10. You read a mixed review of Movie A, but went to see it anyway. You came out of it thinking, "well, it could have been better," because you anticipated it to be mediocre. Apparently, your beliefs about how much you thought you'd like the movie affected your actual experience. This is explained by

    a. the affective expectation model
    b. the self-fulfilling prophecy
    c. illusory correlations
    d. salience

11. John Bargh is known for his research on:

    a. mood-congruent memory
    b. automatic evaluation and activation
    c. illusory correlations
    d. integrating information

12. Daniel Wegner has conducted research in which some participants were asked not to think of a white bear and other participants were given no thought-suppressing instructions. Those who were told not to think of a white bear thought about the white bear more than those who were not so instructed. What is this phenomenon called?

    a. a rebound effect
    b. recurrent thoughts
    c. reactance
    d. none of the above

13. The ways in which people use their emotions to make decisions about the future is:

    a. predictive forecasting
    b. emotional forecasting
    c. future-oriented forecasting
    d. affective forecasting

14. Schemas about extremely common events are called:

    a. scripts
    b. role schemas
    c. event schemas
    d. cognitive schemas

15. The most common or best examples of a schema are:

    a. scripts
    b. prototypes
    c. exemplars
    d. none of the above

16. Sandy meets a nurse, but realizes that she doesn't know much about her except that she is tall and started work at that hospital the day that Sandy was discharged after her minor surgery. When asked to describe her by a friend, what is Sandy most likely to say, when guided by her schema?

    a. I don't know anything about her.
    b. She is absent-minded and doesn't know much about administering medication.
    c. She doesn't like children because I didn't see her with any.
    d. I assume she is warm and caring, and enjoys human service.

17. Which of the following is not an advantage of schematic processing?

    a. schemas aid recall
    b. schemas are affectless
    c. schemas aid automatic inference
    d. schemas speed up processing

18. You learn that Susan likes to sculpt in her spare time, and you also learn that she likes languages. You are asked whether it is more likely that art is one of Susan's majors OR that Susan is an Art/Spanish double major. You say it is more likely that Susan is an Art/Spanish double major. Which of the following explains your response?

    a. the self-fulfilling prophecy
    b. the simulation heuristic
    c. the conjunction error
    d. the affective expectation model

19. Using the ease of remembering examples or the amount of information one can quickly remember as a guide to making an inference is using the:

    a. representative heuristic
    b. conjunction error
    c. simulation heuristic
    d. availability heuristic

20. Because of road construction on your usual route home from work, you decide to go an alternate route. While on this new way home, however, you have an accident. Thinking "If only I had gone the usual way home" is an example of:

    a. simulation heuristics
    b. counterfactual reasoning
    c. mental simulation
    d. representativeness

True-False

Place the letter "T" beside each statement that is true, and place the letter "F" beside each statement that is totally or partially false.

1. The process of social inference consists of several steps.

2. When there are clear standards for combining information into a judgment, a computer typically outperforms a human decision-maker.

3. The way in which decision alternatives are framed can influence people's judgments.

4. Negative moods have a less reliable impact on people's judgments than positive moods.

5. People who try to reappraise negative experiences experience more positive emotions and get along better with people than those who try to suppress negative experiences.

6. The representative heuristic helps one decide if a particular person or event is an example of a particular schema.

7. According to your text, social situations are too varied to allow for effective utilization of an anchoring heuristic.

8. Salience can influence the processing of information in the environment by determining which schemas will be invoked to interpret information that may be subject to multiple interpretations.

9. East Asians are more likely than Westerners to focus on a salient object in their cognitions instead paying attention to the field as a whole.

10. People are less likely to use schemas when they are making decisions under time pressure.

Fill-in-the-Blank

1. A friend tells you that Ingo is uptight and socially awkward. When you first meet Ingo, you are prepared to interact with someone who is reserved, humorless, and stilted, even though Ingo has a lampshade on his head and is telling salty jokes. This is because _____ biased your information gathering about Ingo and his habits.

2. Recalling positive information when you are in a positive mood is an example of _____.

3. People's tendency to consistently overestimate how quickly and easily they will achieve a goal is the _____.

4. _____ is an organized, structured set of cognitions about some concept or stimulus.

5. Matching a specific instance to a larger category often involves _____.

6. Using the ease of imagining other hypothetical outcomes as an indication of the likelihood of these outcomes means employing the _____ heuristic.

7. _____ refers to the property of something standing out from the rest of the background.

8. _____ describes how people sometimes process information in a speedy, effortless way, and sometimes in a careful, deliberate way.

9. The tendency for recently used schemas to be used in unrelated subsequent situations is called the _____.

10. When a person internalizes a perceiver's expectations and comes to believe they are true, a _____ might be the result.

Chapter 4: The Self

Multiple Choice

Circle the letter beside the response that best answers the question or completes the statement.

1. The distinction between having clear ideas about the self and confusion about the self is called:

    a. self-concept
    b. self-esteem
    c. self-verification
    d. self-concept clarity

2. Which of the following refers to the concrete positive or negative evaluations people make of themselves?

    a. implicit self-esteem
    b. explicit self-esteem
    c. self-concept clarity
    d. reflected appraisals

3. _____ refers to the process by which people infer their personal qualities from observing their own behavior.

    a. self-presentation
    b. self-handicapping
    c. self-perception
    d. self-verification

4. Adolescents or young adults who develop only weak ties to both their ethnic culture and the mainstream culture have a _____ identity.

    a. marginal
    b. assimilated
    c. integrated
    d. separated

5. Perceiving oneself as a member of a particular group and behaving in line with that social identity is:

    a. self-stereotyping
    b. schematic processing
    c. bicultural competence
    d. ethnic identity

6. Bicultural competence refers to:

   a. the fact that some individuals can function successfully in both their culture of origin and a new culture
   b. the fact that some individuals may become bilingual if they begin to learn a new language at a young age
   c. the lack of prejudiced and stereotyping behavior found in people who have experienced two cultures
   d. the greater success in a new culture experienced by people with an independent self as opposed to people with an interdependent self

7. The formation and maintenance of a mutually reciprocal interdependent relationship with another person is:

   a. agape
   b. amae
   c. amos
   d. amat

8. People with an independent sense of self are more likely to be motivated by discrepancies between their actual and _____ selves.

   a. ideal
   b. ought
   c. possible
   d. none of the above

9. The ways in which people control and direct their own actions is:

   a. self-presentation
   b. self-handicapping
   c. self-discrepancy
   d. self-regulation

10. An individual's appetitive motivational system corresponds to the:

    a. behavioral activation system
    b. behavioral inhibition system
    c. behavioral motivation system
    d. behavioral distinction system

11. People's need to have a sense of self that is consistent is most in line with which social psychological principle?

    a. self-presentation
    b. self-consistency
    c. self-awareness
    d. self-verification

12. When we are accepted for who we are by people who are important to us, our need to bolster self-esteem may _____.

    a. increase
    b. decline
    c. become more important
    d. help us succeed

13. When a college football player keeps pictures of his favorite players on his wall to inspire him and remind him of the steps he needs to take to reach the same level of success, he is engaging in a process called:

    a. self-presentation
    b. enhancement
    c. self-evaluation
    d. upward comparison

14. Self-_____ needs are especially important following situations of threat or failure.

    a. regulatory
    b. consistency
    c. enhancement
    d. presentation

15. Affirming unrelated aspects of themselves in an effort to cope with specific threats to the self is part of which theory?

    a. self-verification
    b. self-consistency
    c. self-affirmation
    d. self-presentation

16. _____ theory maintains that people are vulnerable to fears about their own mortality and seek ways to mange and minimize the anxiety that this vulnerability causes.

    a. Terror management
    b. Self-affirmation
    c. Self-verification
    d. Social comparison

17. Susan is struggling in her chemistry class. To make herself feel better, she compares herself with other students who are failing the class. Susan is engaging in _____.

    a. upward social comparison
    b. self-verification
    c. self-handicapping
    d. downward social comparison

18. The evaluation of one's life in terms of satisfaction is called

    a. self-comparison
    b. related-attributes similarity
    c. subjective well-being
    d. self-regulation

19. People's tendency to control the impressions that others form of them is _____.

    a. self-verification
    b. self-presentation
    c. self-regulation
    d. self-referencing

20. Publicly announcing our association with successful or powerful people is:

    a. self-promotion
    b. ingratiation
    c. basking in reflected glory
    d. success by association

True-False

Place the letter "T" beside each statement that is true, and place the letter "F" beside each statement that is totally or partially false.

1. People with low self-esteem have a clear sense of what their personal qualities are.

2. Self-schemas describe the dimensions along which a person thinks about himself or herself.

3. Most "possible selves" tend to be positive.

4. According to Yaacov Trope, an accurate sense of self is an important determinant of our selection of a task.

5. According to our findings on the desire for a consistent self, East Asians may view themselves to be more consistent across situations, whereas European Americans may view themselves to be more flexible across situations.

6. People who are low in self-esteem or moderately depressed are more likely to succumb to positive illusions in their self-perceptions.

7. Leon Festinger formulated the initial version of social comparison theory.

8. Virtually any circumstance that makes the self salient can evoke social comparisons.

9. Conveying positive information about one's self to others is known as ingratiation.

10. Modesty boosts a person's public image only when the person's performance has actually been successful.

Fill-in-the-Blank

1. Our perceptions of how other people react to us are called _____.

2. A view of oneself that emphasizes social relations with others and interaction within a larger cultural group is called _____.

3. _____ are more likely than _____ to have an interdependent sense of self and to think of themselves in terms of their relationships with others rather than primarily as independent others.

4. Agitation, fear, and anxiety are aroused when there is a discrepancy between our actual selves and our _____ selves; disappointment, dissatisfaction, and sadness are aroused when there is a discrepancy between our actual selves and our _____ selves.

5. _____ applies in specific situations, and may sometimes be at odds with one's _____, a more general view of one's abilities, motives, and performance.

6. _____ refers to the expectations we hold about our ability to accomplish certain tasks.

7. When people are in a state of _____, they compare themselves to a relevant standard and try to adjust their behavior to conform to that standard.

8. People high in _____ are concerned with identity and how they appear to others, whereas people high in _____ are attentive to their internal states and feelings, and focus attention on the inner aspects of their lives.

9. Jill is a math major in history class. When ranking her own performance in the class, she chooses to compare herself only to people, like herself, who are not history majors. Jill's comparison is based on _____.

10. When we try to control the impressions of ourselves that we give to others, we are practicing _____.

Chapter 5: Attitudes and Attitude Change

Multiple Choice

Circle the letter beside the response that best answers the question or completes the statement.

1. A person's emotions and affect toward the attitude object make up which of the following components of attitudes?

    a. affective
    b. behavioral
    c. cognitive
    d. none of the above

2. Having attractive women paired with automobiles that dealers are advertising on television is using the principle of:

    a. message learning
    b. response involvement
    c. transfer of affect
    d. modeling

3. Which of the following is a primary method by which attitudes are learned?

    a. message learning
    b. transfer of affect
    c. both (a) and (b)
    d. none of the above

4. Balance theory involves all of the following concepts except:

    a. the first person's evaluation of the attitude object
    b. the general utility of the attitude object
    c. the second person's evaluation of the attitude object
    d. the first person's evaluation of the second person

5. The prediction of balance theory that people will change as few affective relations as they can in order to move from imbalance to balance is known as:

    a. propinquity theory
    b. the minimization hypothesis
    c. the least effort principle
    d. the balance principle

6. The aversive state experienced when one is forced to choose between two equally attractive alternatives is:

    a. dissonance
    b. anger
    c. disappointment
    d. contrast

7. Another term for counterattitudinal behavior is:

    a. insufficient justification
    b. attitude-discrepant behavior
    c. assimilation effect
    d. elaboration likelihood

8. According to self-perception theory, which group of participants would rate a boring experimental task the most favorably after telling another participant how much they enjoyed it?

    a. the $1.00 group
    b. the $20.00 group
    c. the control group
    d. the group that worked for the researchers the longest period of time

9. Tricia is buying a car. She has always wanted an SUV. She is trying to decide between a small car or an SUV. According to Tricia, the biggest pro argument of the small car is the gas mileage. The con is the lack of room inside. The biggest pro of the SUV is that it holds all her friends. The con is the gas mileage. She decides that her value of conservation of natural resources is most important, and she expects the small car to meet her needs best. She changes her attitude about small cars and buys one. Which approach did Tricia just take to make her decision?

    a. expectancy-value
    b. discrepancy theory
    c. theory of planned behavior
    d. automatic acquisition

10. Positive or negative thoughts that people have in response to a particular persuasive communication are called:

    a. elaborations
    b. cognitive responses
    c. counterarguments
    d. none of the above

11. Central processing most closely corresponds to which of the following:

    a. heuristic processing
    b. distal processing
    c. dual processing
    d. systematic processing

12. A person who decides that the originator of a discrepant communication is unreliable is engaging in:

    a. source derogation
    b. negative balancing
    c. denial
    d. self-deception

13. At high levels of discrepancy, the maximum amount of attitude change should occur if:

    a. the arguments are weak
    b. the speaker is credible
    c. the issue is very relevant to the listener
    d. no attitude change occurs at high levels of discrepancy

14. When a discrepant position is close to that of the audience, they perceive it as closer than it really is. This process is called:

    a. contrast
    b. association
    c. incorporation
    d. assimilation

15. Repetition is most helpful with:

    a. weak arguments
    b. strong arguments
    c. both (a) and (b)
    d. none of the above

16. Chandra is prevention oriented in her attitude toward dental health. If Byron is attempting to persuade her to floss, which message should be most effective?

    a. "You'll have prettier teeth."
    b. "You can achieve good dental health!"
    c. "It will be cheaper in the long run."
    d. "You can avoid future painful dental procedures."

17. People for whom a message is relevant are most likely to process negative information and change their attitude if they are in a _____ mood.

    a. bad
    b. good
    c. apathetic
    d. neutral

18. The fact that a message from a low-credibility source can sometimes be as effective as that from a high-credibility source is known as:

    a. selective perception
    b. the sleeper effect
    c. the credibility syndrome
    d. the source credibility quotient

19. La Piere's classic study of attitudes revealed that:

    a. there are three components of attitudes
    b. the components of an attitude are different in different cultures
    c. attitudes are learned
    d. there can be major inconsistencies between attitudes and behavior

20. The component that distinguishes the theory of reasoned action from the theory of planned behavior is:

    a. attitudes
    b. subjective norms
    c. behavioral intentions
    d. perceived control

True-False

Place the letter "T" beside each statement that is true, and place the letter "F" beside each statement that is totally or partially false.

1. The cognitive component of an attitude consists of all the person's emotions toward the subject.

2. The "learning theory" approach to attitudes emphasizes the person's subjective experience.

3. Dissonance theory deals especially with inconsistencies between behavior and attitude.

4. Social psychologists use the terms attitude-discrepant behavior and counterattitudinal behavior interchangeably. *T*

5. The greater the amount of choice people have with respect to decisions, the greater the amount of dissonance they should experience. *T*

6. Children, when told that they are strictly forbidden to play with certain toys tend not to devalue the toys when asked to evaluate them afterward. *T*

7. According to research on automatic acquisition and activation, we have a pervasive tendency to nonconsciously classify most, perhaps all, incoming stimuli as either good or bad. *T*

8. Research evidence indicates that under most circumstances, arousing fear decreases the effectiveness of persuasive communications. *F*

9. According to the differential decay hypothesis, the impact of a discounting cue (such as a low-credibility source) on persuasion dissipates less quickly than does the impact of the message itself. *F*

10. Fishbein and Ajzen's reasoned action model assumes that a person's behavior cannot be predicted from his or her behavioral intentions. *F*

Fill-in-the-Blank

1. The three components of an attitude are ____, ____, and ____. *affect, behavioral, cognitive*

2. ____ describes the process by which positive feelings for one stimulus become associated with another stimulus, such as a product or position. *transfer of affect*

3. To restore balance to an unbalanced situation, people typically follow ____. *least effect principle*

4. Self-relevant situations state that dissonance should be experienced primarily by people with ____ rather than ____ self-esteem. *high, low*

5. ____ argues that we interpret our own behavior as an outside observer would, and infer our attitudes from there. *self-perception*

6. ____ refers to generating opposing viewpoints in anticipation of an attitude change message. *counterargument*

7. We tend to be persuaded when a position is adopted by a group of people we like or identify with. Such groups are called ____. *reference group*

8. ____ and ____ are both aspects of the target of an attitude change message. *ego and issue involvement*

9. Attitudes that are __*stable*__ are more likely to predict subsequent behavior.

10. A revision of the reasoned action model is now called the __*theory of planned action*__.

Chapter 6: Prejudice

Multiple Choice

Circle the letter beside the response that best answers the question or completes the statement.

1. The cognitive, affective, and behavioral components of group antagonism, respectively, are:

    a. prejudice, discrimination, stereotyping
    b. stereotyping, discrimination, prejudice
    c. stereotyping, prejudice, discrimination
    d. discrimination, stereotyping, prejudice

2. The knowledge that one is being judged stereotypically and that one might behave in ways that confirm the negative stereotype is:

    a. prejudice
    b. stereotype threat
    c. social learning
    d. a legitimizing myth

3. Overt behavior, such as hiring a white rather than an equally qualified black for a job is called:

    a. prejudice
    b. discrimination
    c. stereotyping
    d. unfair

4. Theories that analyze prejudice as an outgrowth of the particular dynamics of an individual's personality are called:

    a. latent personality theories
    b. conflict theories
    c. stereotyping
    d. psychodynamic theories

31

5. Which of the following statements would a highly authoritarian individual be most likely to endorse?

   a. "Obedience to authority should take second place to an individual's own moral judgment"
   b. "There is nothing too personal to talk about with one's close friends"
   c. "Human nature being what it is, there will always be war and conflict"
   d. "Alternative lifestyles and cultural diversity should be valued and encouraged in society"

6. When two groups are considered unequal, the group with more status may be very affectionate with the subordinate group, and grow emotionally close to them, as long as they "stay in their place." This demonstrates:

   a. legitimizing myths
   b. subtyping
   c. displaced aggression
   d. benevolent paternalism

7. According to the _____, people's attitudes and behaviors are most likely to be guided by their group stereotypes when the target of those attitudes and behaviors conforms to the particular group stereotype.

   a. self-fulfilling prophecy
   b. typicality effect
   c. assumed similarity effect
   d. ingroup favoritism effect

8. Under which of the following conditions are stereotypes most likely to be activated?

   a. when information about an outgroup member is ambiguous
   b. when stereotype-inconsistent behavior is atypical
   c. both (a) and (b)
   d. none of the above

9. Minette keeps her stereotype that blacks are lazy when she sees a successful athlete because she can split blacks into several categories, such as "black athletes" and "black criminals." She is using a process called _____.

   a. subtyping
   b. social identity theory
   c. ambiguity
   d. legitimizing myths

10. Merely being arbitrarily categorized into groups, even without interaction among group members, induced people to show more favorable attitudes toward the in-group than toward the out-group. This was demonstrated through

    a. the outgroup homogeneity effect
    b. the minimal intergroup situation
    c. social identity theory
    d. the theory of optimal distinctiveness

11. Which of the following provides the best example of the ingroup favoritism effect?

    a. assumed similarity effect
    b. optimal distinctiveness
    c. group-serving biases
    d. typicality effect

12. Perceiving the ingroup as more heterogeneous than the outgroup in terms of traits and personality is the:

    a. assumed similarity effect
    b. ingroup favoritism effect
    c. outgroup homogeneity effect
    d. group-serving bias

13. Brewer's theory of optimal distinctiveness suggests that people have which of the following needs?

    a. the need for inclusion in larger collectives
    b. the need for differentiation from other people
    c. both (a) and (b)
    d. none of the above

14. The idea that a decline in old-fashioned racism is more apparent than real and that the only true change has been in people's increased unwillingness to admit prejudicial attitudes is:

    a. symbolic racism
    b. aversive racism
    c. illusory change
    d. latent racism

15. According to the aversive racism perspective, whites may discriminate against blacks only when:

    a. There is another plausible, nonracist justification for their actions.
    b. The consequences of discrimination will be aversive to blacks.
    c. Their racism can be expressed symbolically.
    d. Whites can avoid retaliation by blacks.

16. Stereotypes that involve automatic activation are referred to as:

    a. stereotype threats
    b. explicit stereotypes
    c. implicit stereotypes
    d. minimal intergroup situations

17. Gordon Allport's contact theory of reducing racial prejudice holds that intergroup conflict decreases hostility between the groups only when it meets the condition of:

    a. acquaintance potential
    b. cooperative independence
    c. equal status contact
    d. all of the above

18. A contact technique found to increase peer liking across ethnic and racial groups, to increase the self-esteem of minority children, and to improve academic performance is known as:

    a. cooperative learning
    b. the jigsaw technique
    c. recategorization
    d. cooperative interdependence

19. Which of the following is a cognitive strategy for reducing prejudice?

    a. automatic processing
    b. recategorization
    c. priming
    d. none of the above

20. According to research on cross-cutting categories, in which of these situations would the two students evaluate each other the most negatively?

   a. Jane is in the Iota sorority and Sheila is in the Upsilon sorority. They play together on an intramural softball team.
   b. Jane is in the Iota sorority and Helen is also in the Iota sorority. They play together on an intramural softball team.
   c. Jane is in the Iota sorority and Helen is also in the Iota sorority. Jane and Helen play on competing intramural softball teams.
   d. Jane is in the Iota sorority and Sheila is in the Upsilon sorority. Jane and Sheila play on competing intramural softball teams.

True-False

Place the letter "T" beside each statement that is true, and place the letter "F" beside each statement that is totally or partially false.

1. Virtually every social group is the victim of prejudice at one time or another. **T**

2. Achieving equality has been much more difficult for blacks than for any other minority group. **T**

3. The "authoritarian personality" research falls under the perspective of exchange theory. **F**

4. The theory of realistic group conflict would lead to the expectation of antagonism between the Palestinians and Israelis. **T**

5. Dominant groups create legitimizing myths to explain why the existing social hierarchy must be retained. **T**

6. The value of social identity in enhancing individual self-esteem remains the weakest link in social identity theory. **T**

7. According to your text, "old-fashioned racism" has declined in the United States. **F**

8. According to principled objection critics of symbolic racism, whites oppose affirmative action not because they are racially prejudiced, but because they believe people should be appraised on the basis of their merits. **T**

9. The more formal education people have, the more prejudiced they are likely to be. **T**

10. Recategorization relies on creating superordinate groups. **T**

Fill-in-the-Blank

1. _____ are beliefs about the typical characteristics of group members. *stereotypes*

2. In studies of _____, Asian American women performed better when their Asian identity was cued, but worse when their gender identity was cued, confirming the stereotype of Asians as good at math or the stereotype of women as bad at it. *stereotype threat*

3. The belief that members of one's ingroup are superior to members of all other outgroups is called _____. *ethnocentrism*

4. Unfair treatment of or unjustifiable behavior toward a group and its members is also known as *discrimination*

5. Some have said that affirmative action represents a type of _____ because it favors a minority group at the expense of the majority. *reverse discrimination*

6. If the source of one's annoyance cannot be attacked because of fear or simple unavailability, one may engage in _____ against a substitute target. *displaced anger*

7. _____ are used by a dominant group to explain why a social hierarchy exists and why it must be perpetuated. *legitimizing myth*

8. The distinction between self-interest and group-interest is analogous to the distinction between _____ and _____, according to the theory of relative deprivation. *egotistical and fraternal deprivation*

9. People generally evaluate fellow ingroup members more positively and allocate greater rewards to them, compared to members of the outgroup. This is known as _____. *in-group favoritism*

10. The _____ is the tendency for ingroup members to perceive other ingroup members as more similar to themselves than to outgroup members. *assumed similarity effect*

Chapter 7: Social Influence

Multiple Choice

Circle the letter beside the response that best answers the question or completes the statement.

1. Young people choosing to dress like others in their social group is an example of:

    a. conformity
    b. compliance
    c. legitimate authority
    d. none of the above

2. In Asch's study, _____ of the participants gave an answer that was obviously wrong to them after listening to 4 confederates give that answer.

    a. none
    b. 10%
    c. 35%
    d. 80%

3. People living in _____ cultures tend to emphasize the negative aspects of conformity.

    a. collectivistic
    b. individualistic
    c. both (a) and (b)
    d. none of the above

4. Sherif's classic study of conformity illustrated the power of _____ influence.

    a. authoritarian
    b. informational
    c. normative
    d. minority

5. Conformity due to a desire for social approval is known as:

    a. normative influence
    b. informational influence
    c. individualism
    d. collectivism

6. When conformity is based on the belief that group members are right, we usually:

   a. don't change at all
   b. change our mind, but not our behavior
   c. change our behavior, but not our mind
   d. change our mind and our behavior

7. Asch found that increasing the size of the group past ____ did not increase the amount of conformity for his line judgment task.

   a. 1
   b. 4
   c. 6
   d. none of the above

8. At SMU, in order to promote healthy behavior, a poster advertised that nine out of ten men stop the first time their dates day no to sexual activity. This is an example of:

   a. the desire for individuation
   b. minority influence
   c. majority influence
   d. social norms marketing

9. Double minorities (people who differ from the majority in two ways) are also called:

   a. innovators
   b. in-group minorities
   c. out-group minorities
   d. individuated

10. The base of power identified by Raven that has special relevance to personal relationships and groups is _____.

    a. expertise
    b. legitimate
    c. reward
    d. referent

11. The situation in which an influencer changes the situation so that a target of influence must comply is called a (an):

    a. environmental manipulation
    b. situational manipulation
    c. coercive manipulation
    d. legitimate manipulation

12. The expectation in American culture that people should help those who are less fortunate and, therefore, it is legitimate for those in need to ask for help is known as:

    a. institutionalized welfare
    b. the norm of reciprocity
    c. the norm of social responsibility
    d. the subculture of poverty

13. According to research by Forgas, who is most likely to comply with a request?

    a. people who are angry
    b. people with low self-esteem
    c. people who are in a good mood
    d. people who are in a bad mood

14. A salesperson who tries to increase compliance by inducing an individual to agree first to a small request is using a compliance technique known as the:

    a. foot-in-the-door technique
    b. door-in-the-face technique
    c. low-ball technique
    d. high-ball technique

15. Bargaining is most closely related to which of the following social influence techniques?

    a. foot-in-the-door
    b. door-in-the-face
    c. low-ball
    d. pique

16. The compliance tactic in which a person is asked to agree to something on the basis of incomplete information and is later told the full story is known as the:

    a. low-ball technique
    b. that's-not-all technique
    c. foot-in-the-door technique
    d. door-in-the-face technique

17. Increasing someone's compliance with a request by making a unique request that disrupts his or her refusal script is an example of the _____ technique.

    a. foot-in-the-door
    b. low-balling
    c. door-in-the-face
    d. pique

18. If pressured too strongly to stop drinking, you might feel your personal freedoms are being threatened and therefore may drink more to demonstrate your freedom. This is an example of:

    a. reactance theory
    b. legitimate authority
    c. the low-ball technique
    d. the pique technique

19. In the Milgram study, what percentage of participants gave the highest level of shock?

    a. 0%
    b. 10%
    c. 65%
    d. 85%

20. Miller's suggestion that evil acts are not necessarily performed by abnormal or "crazy" people is called the:

    a. obedience thesis
    b. normality thesis
    c. normalized atrocity thesis
    d. normative thesis

True-False

Place the letter "T" beside each statement that is true and place the letter "F" beside each statement that is totally or partially false.

1. The research of Muzafer Sherif that utilized the judging of lines focused on the nature of conformity in ambiguous situations.

2. In studies similar to Asch's line study, people from collectivist cultures conformed more than people from individualistic cultures.

3. The more we trust the group's information and value their opinions in a situation, the more likely we are to go along with the group.

4. Many experiments have demonstrated that conformity usually increases as the size of the unanimous majority increases.

5. In general, the more committed a person is to a group, the greater the pressures for conformity.

6. A sole dissenter can reduce conformity only if he or she gives correct answers.

7. When people do what they are asked to do, even though they might prefer not to, we call it conformity. **F**

8. Although a dissenting minority can challenge the harmony of group interaction, disagreement may have important benefits for the group. **T**

9. According to Raven, the "power of helplessness" is a form of illegitimate power. **F**

10. In the Milgram study, obedience was highest when participants felt personally responsible for inflicting pain. **F**

Fill-in-the-Blank

1. "Informational social influence" means that we conform to the will of a group because of _____. *information provided by group*

2. Two of the most important reasons to conform are to be _____ and to be _____. *right / liked*

3. _____ refers to all the forces, both positive and negative, that act to keep an individual in a relationship with a group. *commitment*

4. Some people prefer to stand out from the rest of a group. These people might score high on _____. *desire for individuation*

5. According to _____, minority influence and majority influence involve different cognitive processes among group members. *dual process hypothesis*

6. _____ is defined as doing what we are asked to do even though we might prefer not to. *compliance*

7. Using _____ means relying on the ability to provide a negative outcome. *coercion*

8. Using _____ means relying on the persuasive content of a message to induce compliance. *information power*

9. Obedience involves following the orders of _____. *legitimate authority*

10. The _____ technique relies on increasing the desirability of an initial offer. *that's not all*

Chapter 8: Interpersonal Attraction

Multiple Choice

Circle the letter beside the response that best answers the questions or completes the statement.

1. The absence of an intimate attachment figure might produce:

    a. social loneliness
    b. emotional loneliness
    c. social integration
    d. none of the above

2. Research shows that people who experience ostracism showed:

    a. an increase in mood and an increase in self-esteem
    b. an increase in mood and a decrease in self-esteem
    c. a decrease in mood and a decrease in self-esteem
    d. a decrease in mood and an increase in self-esteem

3. When the parent is generally unresponsive or even rejecting, infants and parents are said to have what type of attachment style?

    a. secure
    b. avoidant
    c. anxious/ambivalent
    d. none of the above

4. Adults who seek intimacy but worry that others won't reciprocate their love and won't stay with them have which attachment style?

    a. secure
    b. avoidant
    c. anxious/ambivalent
    d. anxious/avoidant

5. The Westgate West study conducted by Festinger and his colleagues demonstrated which factor that influences interpersonal attraction?

    a. physical attractiveness
    b. similarity
    c. competence
    d. proximity

6. Recent instances in which people have discussed something of personal importance with another person are called:

   a. social exchanges
   b. memorable interactions
   c. memorable exchanges
   d. close relationships

7. Showing a preference for the letters in our own name illustrates:

   a. selective attention
   b. similarity
   c. mere exposure
   d. expectancy-value

8. Which of the following mechanisms has been used to explain why people in close relationships tend to have similar attitudes?

   a. selective attraction
   b. social influence
   c. environmental factors
   d. all of the above

9. People have been able to legally participate in interracial marriage in any state since:

   a. 1991
   b. 1980
   c. 1967
   d. interracial marriage was never banned in any state

10. Approximately what percentage of break-ups described by students involve "fatal attractions" of one kind or another?

    a. 12%
    b. 20%
    c. 30%
    d. 56%

11. Thinking that it will enhance her public image, Susan chooses to hang out with the more physically attractive men in her class. What social psychological principle does Susan's behavior illustrate?

    a. matching principle
    b. radiating effect of beauty
    c. pratfall effect
    d. mere exposure effect

12. Psychological research on the effects of the Internet on people's social relationships have revealed:

    a. that the Internet is bad
    b. that the Internet is good
    c. that the Internet is neither good nor bad
    d. no research has been conducted examining this relationship

13. Studies of college students have found the following sex difference:

    a. A partner's physical attractiveness was considered a necessity by men but a luxury by women.
    b. A partner's status and resources were a necessity for males but a luxury for females.
    c. Men considered kindness and intelligence more important than women did.
    d. Men gave greater emphasis to warmth and trustworthiness than women in a long-term relationship.

14. Which of the following explanations has been offered to explain consistent sex differences in mate selection?

    a. sociocultural theory
    b. evolutionary theory
    c. both (a) and (b)
    d. none of the above

15. Who proposed that men and women have evolved different mating preferences to maximize their reproductive success?

    a. Hatfield
    b. Rubin
    c. Sternberg
    d. Buss

16. The love style in which a person simply seeks contentment rather than excitement is known as:

    a. romantic love
    b. best-friend love
    c. pragmatic love
    d. altruistic love

17. Which of the following is not included within Sternberg's triangular theory of love?

    a. intimacy
    b. passion
    c. attachment
    d. commitment

18. "Puppy love" most closely corresponds to:

    a. empty love
    b. companionate love
    c. fatuous love
    d. infatuated love

19. According to Sternberg, which of the components of the triangular theory of love does "liking" have?

    a. intimacy
    b. passion
    c. commitment
    d. attachment

20. The relationship between dependency and jealousy is:

    a. positive
    b. negative
    c. curvilinear
    d. there is no relationship between dependency and jealousy

True-False

Place the letter "T" beside each statement that is true, and place the letter "F" beside each statement that is totally or partially false.

1. The earliest roots of human affiliation are to be found in adolescence. F

2. All children develop an attachment to their primary caretaker. T

3. Children's attachment has been explained both by innate biological factors and by learning. T

4. Avoidant adults tend to describe their parents as more demanding, critical, and uncaring than anxious/ambivalent and secure adults. T

5. Research has shown that being a good conversationalist enhances a person's likeability. T

45

6. Qualities that initially attract us to someone may turn out to be fatal flaws in the relationship.

7. Anti-fat prejudice is more prevalent in Mexico than in the U.S. F

8. There is a high correlation between measures of individualism and the necessity of love for marriage. T

9. In assessing whether someone loves us, we usually depend not only on their words, but also on their actions. T

10. According to Ellen Berscheid, as a relationship continues over time and interdependence grows, the potential for strong emotion decreases. F

Fill-in-the-Blank

1. When a parent is generally available and responsive to the child's needs, a _____ attachment style develops. *secure*

2. A securely attached child's belief that people are generally trustworthy and responsive is known as her _____ of relationships. *working model*

3. We like people when we perceive our interactions with them to be profitable; the rewards outweigh the costs. This is called _____. *social exchange*

4. Moe lives in Shreveport. Lucy lives in Vancouver. An objective analysis of their traits reveals that the two were "made for each other." However, Moe is in love with the girl next door, and Lucy married the neighborhood butcher. This is an example of _____ in attraction. *proximity*

5. _____ predicts that repeatedly seeing someone in your environment should increase your liking for that thing. *mere exposure*

6. Donn Byrne was able to isolate the effects of similarity of attitudes on liking. He accomplished this using the _____ technique. *phantom other*

7. Personal qualities that initially attract us to someone can occasionally turn out to be _____ in the relationship. *fatal flaws*

8. Attachment, caring, and _____ were the three themes characterizing love, according to Rubin. *trust and self-disclosure*

9. The questionnaire developed by Hendrick and Hendrick measures six ways people commonly define love. They are called _____. *love styles*

10. _____ is the affection we feel for those with whom our lives are deeply intertwined. *companionate love*

Chapter 9: Close Relationships

Multiple Choice

Circle the letter beside the response that best answers the question or completes the statement.

1. According to your text, the most influential perspective on social interaction is:

    a. the norm of reciprocity
    b. *interdependence theory* ✓
    c. functionalist theory
    d. social comparison theory

2. In terms of interdependence theory, _____ are the negative consequences that occur in an interaction or relationship.

    a. punishments
    b. negative reinforcers
    c. *costs* ✓
    d. inhibitors

3. Foa and Foa identified six basic types of rewards that they classified along two dimensions. The dimension that captures the distinction between tangible rewards and symbolic rewards is:

    a. *particularism* ✓
    b. concreteness
    c. symbolicness
    d. none of the above

4. The quality of outcomes a person believes he or she deserves is reflected in the:

    a. comparison level
    b. comparison level for alternatives
    c. *norm of reciprocity* ✓
    d. companionate process

    A

5. People in a relationship who share common interests and goals are said to have:

    a. a high comparison level
    b. correspondent outcomes
    c. *interdependence* ✓
    d. none of the above

    B

47

6. Clusters of rules about how people should behave in a particular type of interaction or relationship are:

   a. social norms
   b. self-disclosures
   c. social roles
   d. role taking

7. The fairness rule that corresponds to distributive justice is:

   a. equality
   b. equity
   c. relative needs
   d. none of the above

8. Which of the following is not an assumption of equity theory?

   a. In a relationship or group, individuals try to maximize their outcomes.
   b. Dyads and groups can maximize their collective rewards by evolving rules or norms about how to divide rewards fairly among everyone concerned.
   c. When individuals perceive that a relationship is inequitable, they feel distressed.
   d. All of these are assumptions of equity theory.

9. Using cognitive strategies to alter one's perception of the imbalance in a relationship is a way of restoring:

   a. equality
   b. actual equity
   c. cognitive equity
   d. psychological equity

10. Which of the following distinguish exchange and communal relationships?

    a. People in communal relationships pay more attention to the needs of their partner.
    b. People in exchange relationships prefer discussing unemotional topics.
    c. People involved in exchange relationships are perceived as more altruistic when they offer help to one another.
    d. All of the above.

11. Revelations that reveal personal opinions and feelings are:

    a. descriptive disclosures
    b. evaluative disclosures
    c. personal disclosures
    d. communal disclosures

12. When people deliberately refrain from talking about themselves to others, they are engaging in:

    a. social validation
    b. social control
    c. self-clarification
    d. self-deprecation

13. The relationship between self-disclosure and liking is:

    a. positive
    b. negative
    c. curvilinear
    d. there is no relationship between self-disclosure and liking

14. Risks of self-disclosure include which of the following?

    a. rejection
    b. betrayal
    c. indifference
    d. all of the above

15. According to studies on self-disclosure and arranged versus love-based marriages, which of the following is supported by research?

    a. Higher satisfaction was associated with lower verbal disclosure in U.S. couples.
    b. In Indian couples in arranged marriages, lower verbal disclosure was associated with lower marriage satisfaction.
    c. The link between self-disclosure and marital satisfaction has little to do with cultural beliefs.
    d. Indian women in love-based marriages were happier when they talked more about personal matters.

16. In cross-cultural studies of power and relationships, this pattern was found:

    a. African-American marriages tend to be matriarchal.
    b. Latino marriages are more patriarchal than African-American and Caucasian marriages.
    c. African-American wives are more powerful than their Caucasian counterparts.
    d. African-American, Latino, and Caucasian marriages demonstrate few overall differences in power.

17. Something that can be used to satisfy or frustrate needs or move persons from or closer to their goals is a _____.

    a. conflict
    b. resource
    c. social norm
    d. aggressive trigger

18. The conflict that focuses on your partner's laziness is which type of conflict?

    a. personal dispositions
    b. social penetration
    c. specific behaviors
    d. norms and roles

19. Lack of attractive alternatives and investments contribute to which of the following types of commitment?

    a. personal commitment
    b. moral commitment
    c. constraint commitment
    d. satisfactory commitment

20. Of Rusbult's common reactions to relationship dissatisfaction, which two are constructive, relationship-promoting responses?

    a. neglect and exit
    b. exit and voice
    c. loyalty and voice
    d. loyalty and exit

True-False

Place the letter "T" beside each statement that is true, and place the letter "F" beside each statement that is totally or partially false.

1. According to interdependence theory, people are usually unaware of the costs and rewards involved in a relationship.

2. What is rewarding for one person may be of little value to someone else.

3. According to Foa and Foa, love is a particularist reward.

4. When partners have different preferences and values, they have "noncorrespondent outcomes" and are more prone to conflicts of interest.

5. Those couples who experienced greater marital distress after the arrival of their baby were less likely to report an inequitable division of housework. **F**

6. According to Clark and Mills, people in "exchange relationships" feel no special responsibility to the welfare of the other person. **T**

7. The relationship between self-disclosure and liking depends, in part, on the meaning attached to a person's revelations and on our own goals in the relationship. **T**

8. In same-sex relationships, women usually disclose significantly more than men. **T**

9. Relationships in which one partner gives more than the other are not as satisfying to partners as balanced relationships. **T**

10. According to Rusbult and her colleagues, the four responses to dissatisfaction are exit, voice, loyalty, and neglect. **T**

Fill-in-the-Blank

1. _____ is a framework used by social psychologists to analyze the patterns of interaction between two partners. **interdependence theory**

2. Assessing how one relationship compares to other relationships currently available to us means considering our _____. **comparison level of alternatives**

3. The principle of _____ argues that each person in a relationship should receive the same outcomes. **equality**

4. _____ theory argues that individuals compare their inputs and outcomes with those of their partner in a relationship to determine their fairness of the relationship. **equity**

5. When Myron does a favor for Lois (e.g., gives her a dollar to buy a soda), he does so without expecting anything in return. This is because they have a _____ relationship. **communal**

6. _____ is a benefit of self-disclosure in a relationship. It allows us to share our feelings and focus our thinking. **self-clarification**

7. According to research in male-female relationships, _____ are more likely than _____ to reveal their weaknesses and to conceal their strengths; _____ showed the reverse pattern of disclosing their strengths and concealing their weaknesses. **women / men / men**

8. _____ results from feelings of understanding, validation, and caring from one's partner. **Intimacy**

9. _____ (*social power*) is a person's ability to influence deliberately the behavior, thoughts, and feelings of another person.

10. "I have to sacrifice or my partner won't love me" is an example of a(n) _____ (*avoidance*) reason for making a sacrifice.

Chapter 10: Behavior in Groups

Multiple Choice

Circle the letter beside the response that best answers the question or completes the statement.

1. A person who is first learning to drive a stick-shift car often finds that he or she is unable to drive and talk to someone else, eat, or listen to the radio. In fact, the presence of someone else in the car can be very distracting and nerve-wracking. What type of response is learning to drive the car?

    a. nondominant
    b. dominant
    c. habitual
    d. facilitated

    [Answer marked: A]

2. The idea that the presence of other people can motivate us because we are concerned about how those others will evaluate us is called:

    a. social inhibition
    b. evaluation apprehension
    c. distraction-conflict
    d. innate arousal

    [Answer marked: b]

3. Jane is not good at logic puzzles, and doubts her own ability to complete the task. She is working on this puzzle in the presence of others. According to the biopsychological explanation, what physiological response should she experience?

    a. challenge
    b. threat
    c. evaluation apprehension
    d. distraction

    [Answer marked: B]

4. Max Ringelmann conducted the initial research on:

    a. social facilitation
    b. group expectations
    c. the distraction-conflict model
    d. social loafing

    [Answer marked: d]

53

5. According to Karau and Williams (1993), how hard an individual works on a group task depends on which of the following?

   a. the person's belief about how important or necessary his or her own contribution is to group success
   b. how much the person values the potential outcome of group success
   c. both (a) and (b)
   d. none of the above

6. In spite of evidence we have for social loafing, people sometimes work harder to compensate for others in their group. What is this phenomenon called?

   a. social compensation
   b. social impact theory
   c. deindividuation
   d. social constructionism

7. The description "Mob behavior is infectious, like a cold spreading among students in a classroom" defines what social phenomenon?

   a. social loafing
   b. crowding
   c. dehumanization
   d. social contagion

8. Which of the following is not a theory of crowding?

   a. sensory overload
   b. social contagion
   c. attributions
   d. loss of control

9. The patterns of behavior, division of labor, and social roles assumed by its members constitute a group's social _____:

   a. cohesiveness
   b. control
   c. functions
   d. structure

10. General attributes of a person, such as age, sex, and ethnicity, that people tend to associate with ability are called:

   a. expectation states
   b. specific status characteristics
   c. diffuse status characteristics
   d. general status characteristics

11. In a (an) _____ task, group productivity is generally superior to the efforts of any one person.

   a. additive
   b. conjunctive
   c. disjunctive
   d. reflective

12. Although a group usually outperforms individuals in an additive task, the group performance is typically less than the sum of the individual inputs. What is one possible explanation for this finding?

   a. social impact
   b. social loafing
   c. groupthink
   d. none of the above

13. The idea of a "weakest link" goes along with which type of task?

   a. additive
   b. conjunctive
   c. disjunctive
   d. compensatory

14. Which of the following is not a rule of brainstorming?

   a. criticism is ruled out
   b. freewheeling suggestions are discouraged
   c. quantity is wanted
   d. combinations and improvements are sought

15. The finding that members of brainstorming groups tend to perform at relatively similar levels is:

   a. compensation
   b. the matching hypothesis
   c. groupthink
   d. social matching

16. A committee is meeting to decide which painting would be more aesthetically pleasing in the office lounge. Both paintings match the color and décor of the lounge; the decision is a matter of opinion. Which decision rule will the group most likely use?

    a. majority-wins
    b. truth-wins
    c. minority-wins
    d. expert-wins

17. The idea that discussion causes individuals to focus on their group membership is the:

    a. social identity process
    b. persuasive arguments perspective
    c. social comparison process
    d. self-presentational process

18. Which of the following is not a characteristic of groupthink?

    a. the group assumes its position is moral
    b. the group stereotypes its opponent
    c. the group encourages disagreeing opinions
    d. the group has an illusion of unanimity

19. When people played the trucking game, most people:

    a. Cooperated and shared the road.
    b. Didn't want to bother the other player, and used the alternative route.
    c. Competed at first, but then learned their lesson and cooperated thereafter.
    d. Competed on nearly every trial.

20. According to research on gender and leadership, women score higher than men on:

    a. trustworthiness
    b. masculinity
    c. transformational leadership
    d. task-oriented leadership

True-False

Place the letter "T" beside each statement that is true, and place the letter "F" beside each statement that is totally or partially false.

1. Social facilitation is a uniquely human phenomenon.

2. Social inhibition is more likely to occur for complex tasks than for simple tasks.

3. Recent research indicates that the phenomenon of social loafing occurs for physical but not intellectual tasks. **F**

4. Social impact theory suggests that the total impact of other people on an individual depends on the characteristics of the source of influence. **F**

5. The critical factor in deindividuation is not membership in a group, but rather anonymity and the size of the group. **T**

6. Crowding doesn't occur when people have plenty of physical space. **F**

7. The persuasive arguments perspective emphasizes that people gain new information as a result of listening to a group's discussion. **F**

8. The basic finding of group polarization research is that group discussion leads to more extreme decisions than those produced by individuals acting alone. **T**

9. When group members are evenly split on an issue, depolarization may occur. **T**

10. When studying culture and competition, researchers have found that as the influence of U.S. cultures and values increases, children tend to become more competitive. **T**

Fill-in-the-Blank

1. All the Whos down in Whoville are singing around the big Who tree, but as it turns out most of them are not singing as loudly as they might be if they were singing while alone. The Whos are demonstrating _____. **social loafing**

2. _____ explains how immediacy, number, and strength of others influences a person's behavior in front of a group. **social impact theory**

3. _____ occurs when there is a weakening of personal responsibility for our actions; it is often produced by being a member of a crowd. **deindividuation**

4. The objective number of people in a certain space is defined as _____. **social density**

5. All the forces, positive and negative, that cause members to remain in a group, are collectively known as _____. **cohesiveness**

6. Group members spend considerably more time discussing shared than unshared information. This phenomenon is called _____. **the common shared knowledge effect**

7. Situations in which the goals are structured in such a way that everybody "sinks or swims" together have a _____ reward structure. **cooperative**

8. A **social dilemma** is a situation in which a desirable choice for the individual results in undesirable consequences for the group.

9. **Task** leadership emphasizes accomplishing the goals of a group, whereas **social** leadership focuses on member interaction.

10. The **contingency model of leadership effectiveness** emphasizes the interaction between a leader's style and the nature of the leadership situation.

Chapter 11: Gender

Multiple Choice

Circle the letter beside the response that best answers the question or completes the statement.

1. Beliefs about the personal attributes of males and females are:

    a. cultural stereotypes
    b. gender stereotypes
    c. institutionalized stereotypes
    d. personal stereotypes

2. The tendency to emphasize men's faces and women's bodies has been called:

    a. stereotyped
    b. gender-ism
    c. body-ism
    d. face-ism

3. Our own unique beliefs about the attributes of groups of people such as women and men are our _____.

    a. cultural stereotypes
    b. personal stereotypes
    c. collective identities
    d. gender identities

4. Research by Williams and Best has found that the core elements of gender stereotypes are _____ across cultures.

    a. quite different
    b. somewhat similar
    c. quite similar
    d. no cross-cultural research has been done on this topic

5. Distinguishing specific categories of women, for example, as mothers, career women, beauty queens, etc. is an example of:

    a. stereotyping
    b. gender typing
    c. personal stereotypes
    d. gender subtypes

6. Which of the following has been found to increase or decrease the influence of stereotypes?

   a. the amount of information available about a person
   b. the salience of the person's group membership
   c. both (a) and (b)
   d. none of the above

7. According to Susan Fiske, why are people in power likely to stereotype?

   a. The powerful don't need to pay close attention to the situation, and therefore don't have the opportunity to disconfirm stereotypes with specific information.
   b. The powerful have more self-confidence than the less powerful, and therefore don't feel as if they need to learn individuating information about employees.
   c. People from prejudiced households are more likely to be elected to positions of power than those from less-prejudiced households.
   d. a and b.

8. On a business trip, you have a meeting scheduled with an executive that you have been told is cold and ruthless. As you initially interact with the executive, you remain distant and aloof, expecting the same from him. Not surprisingly, he behaves exactly as you expected. This example illustrates:

   a. stereotypes
   b. self-fulfilling prophecies
   c. gender typing
   d. congruence

9. Women tend to receive more negative ratings than men in all but which of the following situations?

   a. when they adopt a task-oriented and directive leadership style
   b. when they work in a traditionally masculine job
   c. when they are evaluated on a traditionally feminine task
   d. when they are evaluated by men

10. Compared to their evaluations of women's performance, people are more likely to attribute men's success to:

    a. luck
    b. ability
    c. effort
    d. task difficulty

11. Gender identity is usually acquired:

    a. by age 2 or 3
    b. when the child enters school
    (c.) during adolescence
    d. no one is ever totally sure of their gender identity

    A

12. Instead of viewing gender as simply a male/female dichotomy, some individuals include transsexuals, heterosexual cross-dressers, people who view themselves as both male and female, and others who bend the gender rules of society. These people are called:

    a. transsexuals
    b. continuum thinkers
    (c.) transgendered
    d. role transcenders

13. People who score low on both masculinity and femininity are:

    a. masculine
    b. feminine
    (c.) androgynous
    d. undifferentiated

    D

14. Which of the following argues that to ensure mental health, boys and men should be masculine in their interests and attributes, whereas girls and women should be feminine?

    a. the congruence model
    b. the androgyny model
    (c.) the behavioral model
    d. none of the above

    A

15. Traits, such as emotional, kind, and helpful are called:

    (a.) measures of agency
    b. measures of masculinity
    c. measures of femininity
    d. measures of communion

    D

16. Negative agency corresponds to:

    a. unmitigated communion
    (b.) unmitigated agency
    c. unmitigated masculinity
    d. unmitigated femininity

17. The idea that the many different social experiences of boys and girls lead to relatively enduring sex differences in attitudes, interests, skills, and personalities that continue into adulthood is:

    a. social role theory
    b. socialization theory
    c. social situation theory
    d. none of the above

18. What does our research tell us about conformity and women?

    a. In the majority of the studies, women conformed more often than did men.
    b. Men tend to conform more often than women.
    c. Women conform more often than men if the task is a traditionally feminine task.
    d. Women conformed more often than men in a few studies, but not in the majority.

19. Why do we think that women are better than men at accurately interpreting nonverbal communication?

    a. Women are genetically attuned to be sensitive to nonverbal cues.
    b. Women are expected to be superior in emotional matters, and therefore are better trained in nonverbal communication interpretation.
    c. Women are more relationship-oriented than men, and therefore are more motivated to accurately interpret nonverbal communication.
    d. All of the above are possible explanations.

20. According to your text, perhaps the most dramatic change in this century has been women's increased participation in:

    a. sports
    b. politics
    c. N.O.W.
    d. paid work

True-False

Place the letter "T" beside each statement that is true, and place the letter "F" beside each statement that is totally or partially false.

1. The process of gender typing usually ends in childhood.

2. Studies show that children who watch more television believe more strongly that only girls should wash dishes and help with cooking and only boys should mow the lawn and take out the trash.

3. The less information available about a person, the more likely we are to perceive and react to him or her on the basis of stereotypes. **T**

4. Stereotypes always oversimplify and sometimes are dead wrong. **T**

5. People are constantly examining and evaluating the accuracy of their stereotypes. **T**

6. Research has found that men's success is more often seen as resulting from ability while women's success is attributed to the ease of the task. **T**

7. A full explanation of gender differences must consider both the biological capacities of the sexes and the social environment in which males and females live. **T**

8. Social psychologists emphasize the fact that basic biological differences between the sexes can be greatly increased or reduced by social forces. **T**

9. The options available to people today, both at work and in personal relationships, are restricted much more by gender than in previous generations. **F**

10. There are still more men than women entering college. **F**

Fill-in-the-Blank

1. The process of categorizing things as masculine or feminine is called ____. **gender typing**

2. The belief that women are less competent than men, reinforced through watching TV and seeing pictures of women doing housework and men doing calculations at a desk, is an example of a ____ stereotype. **cultural** ~~gender~~

3. Our thinking about gender can be broken down into smaller units, called ____; examples include tomboy, beauty queen, macho man, or businessman. **gender subtyping**

4. Our knowledge of being male or female is called ____. **gender identity**

5. Jason was born male, but feels that, psychologically, he was born a woman. Jason is an example of a ____. ~~transgender~~ **transsexual**

6. ____ is defined as our perception of having the characteristics that make up conventional gender stereotypes. ~~personal stereotype~~ **gender self-concept**

7. A person high in femininity and high in masculinity would have a gender self-concept classified as ____. **androgynous**

8. A technique for statistically combining the results of several independent studies is called _meta-analysis_; it allows us to form general conclusions about research findings, such as research on gender differences.

9. _Men_ are more aggressive than _women_; in fact, the gap between the sexes is greater for _physical aggression_ than for _verbal aggression_.

10. Men and women differ in what they believe they deserve from a job or a relationship; in other words, there are gender differences in _personal entitlement_.

Chapter 12: Helping Behavior

Multiple Choice

Circle the letter beside the response that best answers the question or completes the statement.

1. Behaviors that are helpful or are designed to help others, regardless of the helper's motives are:

    a. altruistic behaviors
    b. self-serving behaviors
    c. prosocial behaviors
    d. empathic behaviors

2. According to Robert Trivers (1971), natural selection may have favored a disposition to feel guilt and a tendency to enforce mutual helping through social means, such as punishment of those who don't follow group rules. This view explains reciprocal altruism using _____.

    a. a biological emphasis
    b. sociocultural mechanisms
    c. the evolutionary perspective
    d. a and c

3. Rules about fairness and the just distribution of resources fall under which norm?

    a. norm of equality
    b. norm of social responsibility
    c. norm of reciprocity
    d. norm of social justice

4. According to the sociocultural perspective of helping, through what process do people come to learn rules and guidelines for prosocial behavior?

    a. observational learning
    b. reinforcement
    c. punishment
    d. socialization

5. Children will share their toys and candy more when:

    a. parents are in the room
    b. teachers/daycare workers are in the room
    c. they have a great many toys and/or candies
    d. they have been rewarded for sharing

6. Melanie and Susan, two seven-year olds, were playing when Melanie fell down. Susan rushed over to help Melanie. Upon observing this helpful act, Wanda, Melanie's mother, praised Susan by saying that she was a very nice and helpful person. What type of praise was Wanda offering?

   a. dispositional
   b. general
   c. reinforcing
   d. altruistic

7. Observational learning is best associated with:

   a. socialization
   b. punishment
   c. modeling
   d. reciprocity

8. The first step in the decision-making perspective of helping is:

   a. perceiving a need
   b. taking personal responsibility
   c. weighing the costs and benefits
   d. deciding how to help

9. According to Shotland and Huston (1979), which of the following is not one of the cues people use to decide if an emergency exists?

   a. there is a clear threat of harm to the victim
   b. some sort of effective intervention is possible
   c. the victim is helpless and needs outside assistance
   d. all of these are cues that people use

10. What emotion are people most likely to feel if they attribute the cause of another's problems to uncontrollable causes?

    a. sympathy
    b. anger
    c. guilt
    d. neglect

11. Brittany has had a wonderful day. She made an "A" on a very difficult test, and she found out that she had been awarded a scholarship for the following year. Returning to her dorm room after her last class for the day, Brittany witnessed someone fall down the stairs outside the building in which her class was held. She immediately went over to help the individual. What concept best explains why Brittany might have done this?

    a. the negative-state relief model
    b. personal distress
    c. mood-maintenance hypothesis
    d. none of the above

12. The _____ suggests that people in a bad mood may help to relieve their own discomfort.

    a. negative-state relief model
    b. mood-enhancement model
    c. bad mood effect
    d. feel bad effect

13. Which of the following individuals would find it easiest to leave a situation in which a person needed help?

    a. a person high in personal distress
    b. a person high in empathy
    c. both (a) and (b)
    d. none of the above

14. Men are more likely than women to help if:

    a. the victim is another man
    b. the victim is a woman
    c. there is no audience
    d. they know the victim

15. apprehensionOne of the best explanations for the failure of people to help in the Kitty Genovese case is the _____, people's feelings of reduced personal responsibility stemming from the belief that other people will intervene.

    a. bystander effect
    b. apathy
    c. confusion of responsibility
    d. evaluation apprehension

16. Which of the following is not an explanation given, according to a decision-making analysis of prosocial behavior, to explain why the presence of other people inhibits helpfulness?

    a. diffusion of responsibility
    b. ambiguity
    c. fear
    d. evaluation

17. The idea that volunteering provides opportunities for personal growth and enhanced self-esteem is considered to be which function?

    a. understanding
    b. self-protection
    c. values
    d. self-enhancement

18. According to _____ theory, people are motivated to understand why they need help and why others are offering to help them.

    a. psychological reactance
    b. attribution
    c. reciprocity
    d. social exchange

19. The unpleasant psychological state often experienced by older adults who frequently receive assistance is explained by:

    a. reactance theory
    b. attribution theory
    c. self-protection
    d. the mood-maintenance hypothesis

20. Which of the following results has been supported by research on gender and seeking help?

    a. Women are more likely than men to have problems with drug and alcohol abuse, but they are less likely than men to seek help for these problems.
    b. Men are more likely than women to have problems with drug and alcohol abuse, but they are less likely than women to seek help for these problems.
    c. Women are more likely than men to have problems with drug and alcohol abuse, and they are more likely than men to seek help for these problems.
    d. Men are more likely than women to have problems with drug and alcohol abuse, and they are more likely than women to seek help for these problems.

True-False

Place the letter "T" beside each statement that is true, and place the letter "F" beside each statement that is totally or partially false.

1. Prosocial behavior refers to acts performed voluntarily to help someone else when there is no expectation of receiving a reward in any form. F

2. According to evolutionary theorists, any genetically-determined trait that has a high survival value will tend to be passed on to the next generation. T

3. When asked about performing helping behavior in the form of social obligations like lending money to a seriously ill person, Brazilians reported that they would enjoy doing what was expected of them, while Americans reported little enthusiasm for performing these required prosocial acts. T

4. In the Halloween candy experiment, increasing personal responsibility led to increased helping. T

5. Efforts to identify a single personality profile of the "helpful person" have not been very successful. T

6. There is considerable evidence that people are more likely to help others when they are in a good mood. T

7. A teacher who is more likely to help a student to make up for missed classes due to a death in the family than to help a student who went on a trip to the Bahamas is following the principles of attribution theory. T

8. Research shows that people are more likely to offer assistance when others are present. F

9. Religiously committed individuals are less likely to volunteer to help those in need and report donating a larger percent of their incomes to charity. T

10. The experience of receiving help is always a positive one. F

Fill-in-the-Blank

1. Performing an act voluntarily to help someone else when there is no expectation of a reward in any form, except perhaps a feeling of having done a good deed is called _____. altruism

2. The _____ predicts that donating to charity may cheer us up. mood maintenance hypothesis / social influence

3. The norm of _____ predicts that people who are either under-benefited or over-benefited in a helping situation will want to restore equity to the relationship. social justice

69

4. The _____ [learning perspective] argues that help-giving can be successfully modeled for potential helpers.

5. When individuals feel _____ [personal responsibility], they are more likely to help.

6. We are more likely to offer help when we attribute the cause of someone's need as _____ [uncontrollable] rather than _____ [controllable].

7. The link between _____ [positive moods] and helping is more straightforward than the link between _____ [negative moods] and helping.

8. The norm of _____ ~~social justice~~ [negative state relief model] says that we should help those who need our help.

9. Roger and Mick both witness a coworker slip and twist her ankle. Although they both feel strong emotions welling up inside them at the sight of their coworker writhing in agony, only Roger rushes to offer assistance, whereas Mick turns and heads for the lunchroom. A possible explanation for their differences in offering assistance could be that Roger is high in _____ [empathy] whereas Mick is high in _____ [personal distress].

10. The technical term for helping a stranger in distress is _____ [bystander intervention].

Chapter 13: Aggression

Multiple Choice

Circle the letter beside the response that best answers the question or completes the statement.

1. Which theory argues that all aspects of social behavior, including aggression, can be understood in terms of evolution?

    a. psychoanalysis
    b. social learning
    c. sociobiology
    d. learning theory

2. Aggressive acts that are dictated by social norms are considered to be:

    a. acceptable
    b. prosocial
    c. sanctioned
    d. displaced

3. A coach who disciplines a disobedient player is engaging in:

    a. prosocial aggression
    b. antisocial aggression
    c. asocial aggression
    d. sanctioned aggression

4. The relationship between temperature and aggression may reflect the operation of:

    a. anger
    b. attack
    c. frustration
    d. desensitization

5. The theory that frustration always leads to aggression and aggression always follows from frustration is the:

    a. reformulated frustration/aggression hypothesis
    b. original frustration/aggression hypothesis
    c. aggressive behavior theory
    d. none of the above

6. A main mechanism determining human aggressive behavior is:

   a. inherited characteristics
   b. the current circumstance that confronts the person.
   c. past learning
   d. anticipated rewards

7. Bandura's Bobo doll studies demonstrated what principle of learning?

   a. reinforcement
   b. imitation
   c. punishment
   d. none of the above

8. The major source of reinforcement and the chief object of imitation for children are:

   a. peers
   b. parents
   c. siblings
   d. teachers

9. Historically, which region of the United States has led the nation in homicides?

   a. southern
   b. western
   c. eastern
   d. northern

10. The competition among countries for specific territories reflects a specific type of instrumental aggression known as:

    a. asocial aggression
    b. realistic group conflict
    c. sanctioned aggression
    d. limited resource conflict

11. Which of the following factors would be most likely to produce deindividuation?

    a. identifiability
    b. anonymity
    c. self-awareness
    d. structured situations

12. Which of the following terms refers to the idea that violence can be imitated and can spread quickly among people?

    a. contagious violence
    b. mob violence
    c. deindividuation
    d. all of the above

13. Which of the following groups of individuals tends to have greater amounts of aggression anxiety?

    a. women
    b. children from middle-income homes
    c. children from homes where parents used reasoning and the withdrawal of affection
    d. all of the above

14. Which of the following drugs has reduced aggression in experimental studies?

    a. PCP
    b. crack cocaine
    c. methamphetamines
    d. marijuana

15. The most likely targets for displaced aggression are those who are:

    a. weak
    b. less dangerous
    c. both (a) and (b)
    d. none of the above

16. Which of the following have been typical characteristics of school shooters in recent years?

    a. male
    b. children with a history of social problems
    c. a history of being teased or bullied
    d. all of the above

17. The generalizability of laboratory research to the real world is:

    a. internal validity
    b. external validity
    c. experimental relevance
    d. demand characteristics

18. Which of the following is most likely to happen while you are watching a violent television program?

    a. After you see the advertisements, you will remember both the brand and the message better than if the TV program wasn't violent.
    b. After you see the advertisements, you will remember the brand of the advertised product better than the message about the product.
    c. After you see the advertisements, you will remember the message of the product better than the brand.
    d. After you see the advertisements you will NOT remember the brand or the message as well as you would have if you had seen a nonviolent program.

19. In order to reduce demand characteristics in laboratory experiments on media violence, researchers may use a(n) _____ method in the lab.

    a. separated posttest
    b. correlational variable
    c. externally valid
    d. field experiment

20. College men who have raped a woman often do not think they have committed rape because:

    a. women often give drugs to impair men's memories
    b. they didn't understand that forcing a woman to have sex against her will was rape
    c. they thought rape only involved children, and these women were all over the age of 17
    d. they were under the influence of alcohol

True-False

Place the letter "T" beside each statement that is true, and place the letter "F" beside each statement that is totally or partially false.

1. Most violence is committed against spouses, children, and lovers.

2. There is more family conflict and more domestic violence in middle-class than in working-class families.

3. In most cases for an attack or frustration to produce aggressive behavior the person must perceive it as intended to harm him or her.

4. Zimbardo uses the term deindividuation to refer to the same behavior that Tarde called contagious violence.

5. Children who are frequently punished for being aggressive turn out to be less aggressive than other adults.

6. Men experience more aggression anxiety than women. ~~F~~ T

7. The basic principle of displacement is that the more similar a target is to the original source of frustration, the stronger will be the individual's aggressive impulses toward that target. T

8. Both the Surgeon General's Report (1972) and the NIMH Commission (1982) supported the notion that there is a causal relationship between televised violence and aggressive behavior. T

9. Men are more likely to aggress against women in partner relationships than women are likely to aggress against men in those relationships. T

10. Narcissists may be more predisposed to sexual coercion than non-narcissists. T

Fill-in-the-Blank

1. **Anger** refers to aggressive feelings rather than aggressive behavior.

2. Aggressive acts that fall somewhere between antisocial and prosocial aggression are called **sanctioned aggression**.

3. Using aggression, especially in the absence of anger, to attain some practical goal is called **instrumental aggression**.

4. **Deindividuation** refers to the contagious violence sometimes shown by people in a mob, whereas **dehumanization** refers to attributing different beliefs and values to the target of aggression, thereby facilitating aggression for the aggressor.

5. Part of alcohol's contribution to aggression may be the **disinhibiting effects** it produces.

6. **Catharsis** is the idea that aggressive impulses can be reduced by letting off steam.

7. It is far more common for workplace crimes to be committed by **members of the public** rather than by **employees**.

8. A longitudinal study in which children's television viewing is measured during a specific time period and then their aggressive behavior is assessed some years later is an example of **correlational** research.

9. Exposure to violent erotica may contribute to **desensitization**, the formation or hardening of callous or demeaning attitudes toward women.

10. Intimidating verbal activity, requests for sexual activity, unwanted physical contact, and a hostile environment are all manifestations of **sexual harassment**.

Chapter 14: Social Psychology and Health

Multiple Choice

Circle the letter beside the response that best answers the question or completes the statement.

1. What percent of the U.S. population is now overweight or obese?

    a. 20%
    b. 35%
    c. 50%
    d. 75%

2. The psychological study of health considers which of the following?

    a. promoting and maintaining health
    b. preventing and treating illness
    c. improving the health care system and the formation of health policy
    d. all of the above

3. Which of the following is not one of the five sets of beliefs around which the practice of health behaviors center?

    a. subjective norms
    b. response efficacy
    c. self-efficacy
    d. threat to health

4. The belief that one is capable of performing a behavior that will reduce a health threat (e.g., quitting smoking to reduce the threat of lung cancer) is one's sense of:

    a. response efficacy
    b. self-efficacy
    c. outcome efficacy
    d. none of the above

5. Patricia smokes a pack of cigarettes a day. However, since her aunt, who also smoked, died of lung cancer a month ago, Patricia has thought seriously about quitting. If Patricia were to be presented with a persuasive communication about the benefits of being smoke free, she would likely process that communication:

    a. centrally
    b. peripherally
    c. efficaciously
    d. sequentially

6. If you would like to increase the likelihood that the target of your persuasive message buys condoms, what should you do?

    a. have the target person complete a self-affirmation task
    b. scare the target person so she feels like she has to buy them
    c. become friends with the target person
    d. combine the condom message with an anti-smoking message

7. Which of the following events is very likely to be appraised as stressful?

    a. negative or unpleasant events
    b. unresolvable events
    c. uncontrollable or unpredictable events
    d. all of the above

8. The relationship between prolonged exposure to stress and prosocial behavior is:

    a. positive
    b. inverse
    c. small
    d. there is no relationship at all between stress and prosocial behavior

9. The most distressing daily hassles are:

    a. lateness
    b. interpersonal conflicts
    c. traffic jams
    d. household responsibilities

10. Trying to control your anger with your significant other or trying to feel less sad when someone has hurt your feelings are examples of:

    a. confrontative coping
    b. avoidance
    c. problem-solving coping
    d. emotion-focused coping

11. Which of the following is not an active coping method?

    a. seeking information
    b. planning
    c. acceptance
    d. attempting to get help from others

12. In Japan, _____ predicted a better pregnancy outcome than any of the other coping strategies.

    a. personal influence
    b. acceptance
    c. confluence
    d. social assurance [circled]

13. Which of the following is considered by researchers to be an indication of successful coping?

    a. the reduction of physiological arousal
    b. the person returns quickly to his or her previous life activities
    c. the reduction of psychological distress
    d. all of the above [circled]

14. Which of the following variables would be associated with a more distressing appraisal of a stressful situation?

    a. dispositional optimism
    b. neuroticism [circled]
    c. conscientiousness
    d. hardiness

15. Which of the following is not a type of social support?

    a. instrumental aid
    b. the provision of information [circled]
    c. emotional concern
    d. all of the above are types of social support

16. Social support is considered by some to be most effective when it is:

    a. direct [circled]
    b. in proportion to need
    c. "invisible"
    d. parcelled out slowly

17. Which of the following variables influences the recognition and interpretation of symptoms?

    a. mood
    b. satisfaction with work and home
    c. expectations
    d. all of the above [circled]

18. Organized, cognitive pictures of one's symptoms that influence one's illness-related activities are:

    a. cognitive maps
    b. sick guides
    c. illness stereotypes
    d. illness schemas

19. Illnesses that are short in duration with no long-term consequences and that are believed to be caused by specific viral or bacterial agents are:

    a. chronic illnesses
    b. acute illnesses
    c. terminal illnesses
    d. cyclic illnesses

20. Patients are most likely to adhere to physicians' medical advice if the treatment

    a. is "medical," like a prescription pill
    b. is an over-the-counter remedy
    c. involves a complex combination of medication
    d. continues over several months

True-False

Place the letter "T" beside each statement that is true, and place the letter "F" beside each statement that is totally or partially false.

1. Currently, the major health problems faced by citizens of industrialized nations are those associated with infectious disease. F

2. In Hispanic cultures, anticipated social support or its absences is a better predictor of health habits than are health attitudes. T

3. Repeated exposure to stressful events has no negative effect on physiological systems. F

4. Research has shown that everyone perceives the same events as stressful. F

5. Confrontation has been shown to be more effective than avoidance in managing stress. T

6. Research demonstrates that social support effectively reduces psychological distress during stressful times. T

7. The first phase of stress management programs for college students involves training the students to observe their own behavior and to record the circumstances they find most stressful. T

8. The flu is an example of a cyclic illness. F

9. When people are asked what is important to them in their medical care, they rate the technical quality of the care as being much more important than the manner in which the care is given. F

10. Chronic disease can confer positive as well as negative outcomes. T

Fill-in-the-Blank

1. *health behaviors* are actions undertaken by people who are healthy to enhance or maintain their health.

2. Fluoridating water and improving dental health care are examples of *health protection programs* advocated by the U.S. Department of Health and Human Services.

3. *health beliefs* refer to a set of attitudes that contribute to the practice of health behaviors.

4. A non-exerciser who believes that exercise alone will not reduce the risk of a particular illness is exhibiting *low* response efficacy.

5. Minor stressful events may have a cumulative impact on health. These are called *daily hassles*.

6. *Coping* is the process of managing demands that are viewed as taxing or exceeding our resources.

7. *dispositional optimism* is a general belief that good outcomes will occur in life; it is one of several coping styles.

8. *hardiness* is a set of attitudes that makes people stress resistant, including a sense of commitment, a positive response to challenge, and an internal sense of control.

9. Providing liking, love, or empathy can be a means of social support; specifically, this refers to *emotional concern* as a social support mechanism.

10. *Cyclic illness* is characterized by alternating periods of symptoms and no symptoms.

Chapter 15: Social Psychology and the Law

Multiple Choice

Circle the letter beside the response that best answers the question or completes the statement.

1. According to research by Brigham, Maass, Snyder, and Spaulding, clerks misidentified the confederates with whom they had been interacting two hours previously what percentage of the time?

    a. 16%
    b. 23%
    c. 56%
    d. 65%

2. Which of the following is not an estimator variable?

    a. viewing opportunity
    b. stress and arousal
    c. lineup biases
    d. weapon focus

3. Variables that concern the eyewitness and/or the situation in which an event was witnessed are:

    a. process variables
    b. system variables
    c. source-monitoring variables
    d. estimator variables

4. The process of perceiving and interpreting information is:

    a. acquisition
    b. encoding
    c. storage
    d. retrieval

5. What effect does the experience of stress typically have on one's memory for an event?

    a. the accuracy of one's memory for the incident itself remains unchanged
    b. the accuracy of one's memory for events leading up to the incident decreases
    c. the accuracy of one's memory for events following the incident decreases
    d. all of the above

6. Which of the following most closely corresponds to the outgroup homogeneity effect?

    a. weapon focus effect
    b. own-race bias
    c. lineup biases
    d. aversive racism

7. Which of the following variables has been shown to decrease the own-race bias?

    a. in-group cohesiveness
    b. viewing opportunity
    c. cross-racial contact
    d. none of the above

8. People often have trouble identifying where they have learned various pieces of information. Thus, they may mistakenly conclude that certain pieces of information came from a source that was not their true origin. This is known as the:

    a. overwriting hypothesis
    b. source-origin hypothesis
    c. source-monitoring theory
    d. forgetting hypothesis

9. Eyewitnesses make the most accurate identifications when they are presented with:

    a. show-up lineups
    b. standard lineups
    c. simultaneous lineups
    d. sequential lineups

10. In order to gain accurate information from eyewitnesses, it is recommended that police officers use phrases such as this one during interviews:

    a. The perpetrator will definitely be in the lineup.
    b. Did you see the perpetrator's knife?
    c. I understand you saw Car A crash into Car B.
    d. What did you see at the crime scene?

11. People who feel pressured to confess to a crime they did not commit but who privately continue to believe in their own innocence display which type of false confession?

    a. voluntary false confessions
    b. coerced compliant false confessions
    c. coerced internalized false confessions
    d. coerced externalized false confessions

12. One technique commonly used by police officers to determine if someone is lying is the:

    a. lie detector test
    b. polygraph test
    c. control question test
    d. all of the above

13. The process during which judges and attorneys question potential jurors about opinions or biases that could adversely affect their ability to render a fair verdict is:

    a. peremptory challenges
    b. death qualification
    c. voir dire
    d. suggestive questioning

14. Attorneys who believe that a potential juror has personality characteristics that might work against their case can choose to exclude that individual from further consideration. What is this process called?

    a. peremptory challenges
    b. death qualification
    c. preemptory challenges
    d. voir dire

15. Individuals who _____ the death penalty are more likely to convict than individuals who _____ the death penalty.

    a. support/oppose
    b. oppose/support
    c. support/are uncertain
    d. none of the above

16. Susan sits on the jury for a capital murder trial. As she hears testimony from the defendant and from witnesses for the prosecution and the defense, she creates a story about the information. According to Hastie and Pennington, what is this called?

    a. narrative methodology
    b. story model
    c. personal fable
    d. cognitive model

17. The idea that jurors reach verdicts through actively interpreting and evaluating the evidence they are given is the:

    a. narrative methodology
    b. story model
    c. personal fable
    d. cognitive model

18. A large amount of pretrial publicity:

    a. increases the likelihood that jurors will convict criminal suspects
    b. decreases the likelihood that jurors will convict criminal suspects
    c. does not affect jurors' decision-making processes
    d. has no bearing on civil cases

19. The theory that most people in contemporary U.S. culture believe in equality but still have some negative beliefs and feelings about blacks is:

    a. aversive racism
    b. symbolic racism
    c. old-fashioned racism
    d. marginal racism

20. _____ juries discuss the trial more thoroughly than other types of juries, and therefore make better judgments about the case.

    a. verdict-driven
    b. evidence-driven
    c. character-driven
    d. leniency-driven

True-False

Place the letter "T" beside each statement that is true, and place the letter "F" beside each statement that is totally or partially false.

1. Research has shown that individuals who witnessed an event under poor viewing conditions were just as likely to make an identification as individuals who witnessed an event under better viewing conditions.

2. The own-race bias tends to be stronger in black individuals than in white individuals.

3. Eyewitnesses make the most accurate identifications with simultaneous lineups.

4. The more confident eyewitnesses are about their testimony, the more accurate their testimony tends to be.

5. A confession is one of the most powerful pieces of evidence that can be presented in court. T

6. Observers are very good at detecting when other people are lying. F

7. Research shows that looking away during an interview indicates that a suspect is lying. F

8. Research shows that high SES defendants are less likely to be found guilty than low SES defendants. ~~F~~ T

9. Smaller juries engage in more extensive deliberations than larger juries. F

10. Juries appear to have a leniency bias in which lower standards are used for deciding to acquit than for deciding to convict a defendant. F

Fill-in-the-Blank

1. __system variables__ are factors that are under the direct control of the criminal justice and/or legal system.

2. The process of recalling information that is stored in memory is __retrieval__.

3. While being robbed in his small store, Dean remembered more about the gun than he did about the perpetrator. This phenomenon is called the __weapon focus effect__.

4. The fact that witnesses tend to be more accurate in identifying individuals who are members of their own race than in identifying those of another race is the __own-race bias__.

5. In __sequential__ lineups, potential perpetrators are shown one at a time, and witnesses must decide whether one person is the perpetrator before seeing the next person.

6. Downplaying the significance of a crime in order to increase the likelihood of confession is called __minimization__.

7. __voir dire__ is the process during which judges and attorneys question potential jurors about opinions or biases that could adversely affect their ability to render a fair verdict.

8. In capital cases, voir dire is often used to eliminate potential jurors who do not support the death penalty, a process known as ~~preemptory challenges~~ __death qualification__.

9. A witness who claims a defendant is too nice to commit a serious crime is providing __character testimony__ evidence.

10. Social psychologists are frequently asked to testify about research findings to give judges and jurors a ~~expert witness~~ __framework__ for understanding and evaluating the evidence in a particular case.

Chapter 1: Theories and Methods in Social Psychology

Multiple Choice

1. (a) The individual level of analysis is typically used by clinical and personality psychologists, who explain behavior in terms of a person's unique life history and psychological characteristics. (p. 3)

2. (d) The frustration-aggression hypothesis predicts that when people are blocked from achieving a desired goal, they feel frustrated and angry and are more likely to lash out. (p. 4)

3. (d) The focus of Gestalt theorists is the way individuals perceive and understand objects, events, and people. In their view, people perceive situations or events not as made up of many discrete elements, but rather as "dynamic wholes." (p. 5)

4. (b) People's needs frequently motivate and influence their perceptions, attitudes, and behavior. Students feel a need to belong when they begin a new school experience, and that desire often motivates them to join clubs and attend events. (p. 6)

5. (c) Cheerleaders capture our attention because there are only a few of them and they are dressed in unique colorful clothing, yell throughout the game, and move around. We recognize them as figures against the ground because they are so easy to separate from the rest of the activity occurring around them. (p. 8)

6. (d) Interdependence means that the outcomes one person receives depend at least in part on the behavior of another person and vice versa. (p. 9)

7. (b) The term social role refers to the set of norms that apply to people in a particular position, such as teacher or student. (p. 11)

8. (c) Collectivist cultures emphasize loyalty to the family, adherence to group norms, and the preservation of harmony in social relations with members of one's own group. (pp. 11-12)

9. (b) Many human tendencies and preferences are the result of natural selection. These are known as evolved psychological mechanisms. They can be seen as adaptive responses to specific problems that were encountered by our ancestors. (p. 13)

10. (b) Social psychologists often develop theories that account for a certain limited range of phenomena. These are called middle-range theories. (p. 14)

11. (d) Social psychological research has four broad goals. In addition to the three listed here, a fourth is theory building. (p. 15)

12. (d) A random sample means that each person in the larger population to which we wish to generalize has an equal chance of being included in the study. (p. 15)

13. (a) College sophomores are used often in social psychology research because they are a readily available population. (p. 16)

14. (b) Rejection is the independent or manipulated variable because the researcher has created different levels of it. (p. 19)

15. (c) Both experimental and correlational research can be done in either the laboratory or the field. (pp. 20-21)

16. (b) External validity reflects the fact that the results of a study are more likely to be valid in situations outside the specific research situation itself. (p. 22)

17. (c) There are two solutions to the problem of experimenter bias. One is to keep the people who actually conduct the research uninformed or blind about the hypotheses or experimental condition to which a subject was assigned. A second solution is to standardize the situation in every way possible. (pp. 24-25)

18. (b) Negativistic subjects try to sabotage experiments. (p. 25)

19. (c) In a conceptual replication, different research procedures are used to explore the same conceptual relationship. (p. 27)

20. (d) The committee of researchers responsible for ensuring that all research is conducted according to a set of general principles laid down by the federal government is an institutional review board. (p. 28)

True-False

1. T (p. 3)
2. T (p. 4)
3. F (p. 5)
4. T (p. 9)
5. F (p. 17)
6. F (p. 19)
7. T (pp. 20-21)
8. F (p. 21)
9. F (p. 21)
10. T (pp. 29-30)

Fill-in-the-Blank

1. Behaviorism (p. 5)
2. individualism (p. 11)
3. Evolutionary social psychology (p. 13)
4. Theories (p. 15)
5. reverse-causality (p. 18)
6. third variable (p. 18)
7. random assignment (p. 20)
8. internal validity (p. 21)
9. Archival research (p. 23)
10. Internet research (p. 24)

Chapter 2: Person Perception

Multiple Choice

1. (d) Salient stimuli produce the most extreme evaluative judgments, are seen as the most causally powerful, and produce more consistency of judgment. (p. 35)

2. (b) Implicit personality theory refers to the fact that certain traits seem to go along together. (p. 35)

3. (c) Dual processing refers to the distinction between category-based impressions and more individuated impressions. (p. 37)

4. (b) When individuals are processing information about another person at a relatively superficial or stereotypic level, assimilation is more likely. (p. 38)

5. (a) Assimilation refers to the biasing of a judgment in the same direction as a contextual standard. Being interviewed simultaneously with a highly competent other should increase the interviewer's perception of your competence. (p. 38)

6. (c) According to Anderson's weighted averaging model, people form an overall impression by averaging all traits but giving more weight to those they feel are most important. The negativity effect would suggest that a negative trait affects impressions more than a positive trait (i.e., egocentric). (p. 40)

7. (c) A prototype is an abstract ideal of a schema. (p. 42)

8. (c) Social perceivers often use rapid, heuristically based processing when their inferences are not particularly important to them, but they are able to switch to the more systematic style of processing when inferences are important. (p. 43)

9. (b) When we are busy or preoccupied, we are more likely to see other people's personal qualities as stable and enduring dispositions. (p. 44)

10. (c) According to Jones and Davis's correspondent inference theory, there are several cues that people use to determine whether a person's behavior reflects an underlying disposition: social desirability, choice, and social role. (pp. 46-47)

11. (b) Covariation refers to people's attempts to see if a particular effect and a particular cause go together across different situations. (p. 48)

12. (a) Kelley's theory suggests that people use distinctiveness information, consensus information, and consistency information when trying to arrive at a causal attribution. (pp. 48-49)

13. (a) The actor-observer effect refers to the tendency for actors to infer situational causes for their own behavior and dispositional causes for others' behavior. (p. 51)

14. (d) The tendency to exaggerate how common one's own opinions or behaviors are is the false consensus effect. (p. 51)

15. (a) The tendency to underestimate others' standing on attributes that make one distinctive is the false uniqueness effect. (p. 52)

16. (c) The tendency to take credit for success (i.e., attributions to ability or effort) and to deny responsibility for failure (i.e., attributions to the teacher or to bad luck) is known as the self-serving attributional bias. (p. 52)

17. (d) It is easiest to distinguish emotions that are at least 3 points apart on Woodworth's continuum. (p. 56)

18. (d) The visible channel of communication includes distance, gestures, and eye contact. (pp. 57-58)

19. (b) Variations in speech are called paralanguage. (p. 59)

20. (d) Nonverbal leakage includes such behaviors as biting the lower lip and blinking more than usual. (pp. 59-60)

True-False

1. T (p. 33)
2. T (p. 39)
3. F (p. 38)
4. F (p. 39)
5. F (pp. 40-41)
6. T (p. 46)
7. T (p. 50)
8. F (p. 52)
9. T (p. 53)
10. T (p. 56)

Fill-in-the-Blank

1. salient (p. 34)
2. Implicit personality theory (p. 35)
3. contrast (p. 38)
4. important (p. 40)
5. the halo effect (pp. 40-41)
6. the discounting principle (p. 48)
7. self-serving attributional bias (p. 52)
8. pragmatic accuracy (p. 55)
9. Interpersonal distance (p. 57)
10. nonverbal leakage (pp. 59-60)

Chapter 3: Social Cognition

Multiple Choice

1. (b) Social cognition is the study of how people form inferences from the social information in the environment. (p. 65)

2. (d) Any social inference is composed of several steps: gathering information, deciding what information to use, and integrating the information into a judgment. (p. 66)

3. (a) Statistical information provides data about a large number of individuals. (pp. 67-68)

4. (b) Negative information attracts more attention than positive information. (p. 68)

5. (c) People are concerned about figuring out "what goes with what" in social life. Many of people's beliefs about what goes with what involve statements about the relationship between things. Such ideas about the associations between things are called judgments of covariation. (p. 69)

6. (c) Illusory correlations can be produced by associative meaning, in which two items are seen as belonging together because they "ought" to be based on prior expectations. Most people expect that bizarre things happen on nights of the full moon, prompting an increased number of emergency room admissions. (p. 70)

7. (c) Several factors can produce an illusory correlation, including associative meaning and paired distinctiveness. (p. 70)

8. (b) Remembering information that fits the valence of one's current mood state is mood-congruent memory. (pp. 71-72)

9. (b) When in a negative mood, fearful people make risk-averse choices and express pessimism about risk, while angry people express more optimistic risk estimates and make risk-seeking choices, like happy people. (p. 72)

10. (a) According to the affective expectation model (AEM), people's beliefs about how they will feel are as important in determining their reactions as are the experiences they actually have. (p. 72)

11. (b) John Bargh is known for his research on automatic evaluation and automatic activation. (pp. 73-74)

12. (a) Being told not to think of a white bear is the same as being told to suppress your thoughts of a white bear. Suppressing one's thoughts is difficult and many of these efforts not only fail but may actually produce a rebound effect, such as thinking about the white bear even more frequently. (p. 75)

13. (d) Affective forecasting refers to the ways in which we use our emotions to make decisions about the future. (p. 76)

14. (a) Schemas about extremely common events are scripts. A script is a standard sequence of behavior over a period of time. (p. 78)

15. (c) Exemplars are the most common or best examples of a schema. (p. 79)

16. (d) Schemas add information. A schema can help us fill in missing information when there are gaps in our knowledge. (p. 81) Choice d fits the typical schema for a nurse.

17. (b) There are many advantages of schematic processing, including that schemas aid information processing, aid recall, speed up processing, aid automatic inference, add information, aid interpretation, provide expectations, and contain affect. As the latter advantage implies, schemas are not affectless. (pp. 80-82)

18. (c) The conjunction error occurs because people believe that the combination of two events is more likely than either of the events alone. They fall back on the representativeness heuristic and ignore statistics. (pp. 82-83)

19. (d) Using the ease of remembering examples or the amount of information one can quickly remember as a guide to making an inference is using the availability heuristic. (pp. 83-84)

20. (b) Counterfactual reasoning refers to the process by which abnormal or exceptional events (e.g., having an accident when taking a new route home) lead people to imagine alternatives that are normal (e.g., if only I had taken my usual route, this would not have happened). (p. 85)

True-False

1. T (p. 65)
2. T (p. 68)
3. T (p. 70)
4. T (p. 72)
5. T (pp. 75-76)
6. T (pp. 82-83)
7. F (p. 86)
8. T (pp. 87-88)
9. F (p. 89)
10. F (p. 91)

Fill-in-the-Blank

1. prior expectations (p. 66)
2. mood-congruent memory (pp. 71-72)
3. planning fallacy (p. 76)
4. A schema (p. 78)
5. the representativeness heuristic (p. 82)
6. simulation (p. 84)
7. Salience (pp. 87-88)
8. Priming effect (pp. 88-89)
9. dual-process model (p. 90)
10. self-fulfilling prophecy (p. 92)

Chapter 4: The Self

Multiple Choice

1. (d) The distinction between having clear ideas about the self and confusion about the self is called self-concept clarity. (p. 97)

2. (b) Explicit self-esteem refers to the concrete positive or negative evaluations people make of themselves. (p. 98)

3. (c) Self-perception refers to the process by which people infer their personal qualities from observing their own behavior. (p. 100)

4. (a) Adolescents or young adults who develop only weak ties to both their ethnic culture and the mainstream culture have a marginal identity. (p. 102)

5. (a) Perceiving oneself as a member of a particular group and behaving in line with that social identity is self-stereotyping. (p. 103)

6. (a) Individuals may be able to gain competence within two cultures without losing cultural identity and without having to choose one culture over the other. This notion of bicultural competence has been related to successful functioning in both one's culture of origin and the new culture. (p. 103)

7. (b) Amae is a Japanese word for the sense of being lovingly cared for and dependent on another's indulgence. (p. 106)

8. (a) People with an independent sense of self are more likely to be motivated by discrepancies between their actual and ideal selves. (p. 110)

9. (d) Self-regulation refers to the ways in which people control and direct their own actions. (p. 110)

10. (a) Psychologists have suggested that people have two independent motivational systems that control what tasks they approach and what tasks they avoid. The appetitive system is known as the behavioral activation system. (p. 112)

11. (d) The process by which people seek out and interpret situations that confirm their already-existing self-conceptions, and avoid or resist situations and feedback that are at odds with their existing self-conceptions is self-verification. (p. 114)

12. (b) When we are accepted for who we are by people who are important to us, our need to bolster self-esteem may decline. (p. 115)

13. (d) A college football player may keep pictures of his favorite players on his wall to inspire him and remind him of the steps he needs to take to reach the same level of success. This process is called upward comparison. (p. 116)

14. (c) Self-enhancement needs are especially important following situations of threat or failure. (p. 116)

15. (c) Affirming unrelated aspects of themselves in an effort to cope with specific threats to the self is part of self-affirmation. (p. 119)

16. (a) Terror management theory maintains that people are vulnerable to fears about their own mortality and seek ways to manage and minimize the anxiety that this vulnerability causes. (p. 120)

17. (d) Downward social comparison is the process by which one compares oneself with others who are less fortunate, less successful, or less happy. (p. 123)

18. (c) The evaluation of one's life in terms of satisfaction is called subjective well being. (p. 125)

19. (b) Self-presentation refers to people's tendency to control the impressions others form of them. (p. 127)

20. (c) Basking in reflected glory (BIRGing) is when we publicly announce our association with successful or powerful other people. (p. 128)

True-False

1. F (pp. 97-98)
2. T (p. 108)
3. T (p. 108)
4. T (p. 114)
5. F (p. 115)
6. F (p. 116)
7. T (p. 122)
8. T (p. 122)
9. F (p. 127)
10. T (p. 128)

Fill-in-the-Blank

1. reflected appraisals (p. 100)
2. interdependent self (p. 104)
3. Women/men (p. 104)
4. ought/ideal (p. 109)
5. Working self-concept/stable self-concept (pp. 110-111)
6. Self-efficacy (p. 111)
7. self-awareness (p. 113)
8. public self-consciousness/ private self-consciousness (p. 113)
9. related-attributes similarity (p. 125)
10. self-presentation (p. 127)

Chapter 5: Attitudes and Attitude Change

Multiple Choice

1. (a) The affective component of attitudes consists of a person's emotions and affect toward an attitude object. (p. 133)

2. (c) Learning theory suggests that people are persuaded when they transfer an affect from one object to another that is associated with it. (p. 135)

3. (c) Learning theory accounts of attitude change and persuasion emphasize two main methods by which attitudes may be acquired or changed: message learning and transfer of affect. (p. 135)

4. (b) There are three relevant evaluations in balance theory: (1) the first person's evaluation of the other person, (2) the first person's evaluation of the attitude object, and (3) the other person's evaluation of the attitude object. (p. 136)

5. (c) Balance theory uses a least effort principle to predict the direction of attitude change. People tend to change as few affective relations as they can to move from imbalance to balance. (p. 137)

6. (a) Dissonance is an aversive motivational state that may follow from having to choose between two equally attractive alternatives. (p. 138)

7. (b) Counterattitudinal behavior and attitude-discrepant behavior are often used interchangeably. (p. 140)

8. (a) Self-perception theory would predict that those participants paid $1.00 would rate the experimental task more favorably. (p. 142)

9. (a) Expectancy-value theory assumes that people adopt a position based on their thoughtful assessment of its pros and cons, that is, on the values they place on its possible effects (p. 143).

10. (b) Cognitive responses are defined as positive or negative thoughts people have in response to a persuasive communication. (p. 144)

11. (d) Central processing most closely corresponds to systematic processing in that both involve careful review and consideration of arguments. (p. 145)

12. (a) A person who decides that the originator of a discrepant communication is unreliable is engaging in source derogation. (pp. 149-150)

13. (b) At high levels of discrepancy, the maximum amount of attitude change should occur if the speaker is credible. (p. 150)

14. (d) Assimilation is the process by which a discrepant position that is close to an audience appears closer than it really is. (p. 151)

15. (b) Repetition helps strong arguments because people process them more completely. But it may hurt weak arguments because it exposes their flaws. (p. 151)

16. (d) Messages may be more persuasive if they match the regulatory leanings of a participant. Therefore, if someone is trying to persuade you to floss and you are prevention oriented, then arguments that stress how you can avoid painful dental procedures may appeal to you. (p. 152)

17. (b) Under positive mood, people for whom the message was relevant were more likely to process negative information and to change their attitude than those in a neutral mood. (p. 156)

18. (b) The sleeper effect refers to a rebound in the persuasiveness of a low credibility source's message. (p. 160)

19. (d) La Piere's classic study of attitudes revealed that there can be major inconsistencies between attitudes (e.g., anti-Asian) and behavior (e.g., accepting Chinese as guests in hotels and restaurants). (pp. 160-161)

20. (d) The revision of the reasoned action model (i.e., the theory of planned behavior) includes perceived control over outcomes as an additional element. (p. 166)

True-False

1. T (p. 133)
2. F (p. 135)
3. T (p. 138)
4. T (p. 140)
5. T (p. 140)
6. T (p. 140)
7. T (p. 146)
8. F (pp. 153-154)
9. F (p. 160)
10. F (p. 165)

Fill-in-the-Blank

1. affective/behavioral/cognitive (p. 133)
2. Transfer of affect (p. 135)
3. the principle of least effort (p. 137)
4. high, low (p. 141)
5. Self-perception theory (p. 142)
6. Counterarguing (p. 144)
7. reference groups (pp. 148-149)
8. Ego involvement/issue involvement (pp. 154-155)
9. stable (p. 162)
10. theory of planned behavior (p. 166)

Chapter 6: Prejudice

Multiple Choice

1. (c) The cognitive, affective, and behavioral components of group antagonism respectively are stereotypes, prejudice, and discrimination. (p. 170)

2. (b) Knowing that one is being judged stereotypically, that one might behave in ways that will confirm the negative stereotype, and that the stereotype might provide a plausible explanation for one's own poor performance has been called stereotype threat. (p. 171)

3. (b) Discrimination is the behavioral component of group antagonism. It consists of negative behaviors (e.g., hiring a white rather than an equally qualified black for a job) toward individuals based on their group membership. (p. 174)

4. (d) Psychodynamic theories analyze prejudice as an outgrowth of the particular dynamics of an individual's personality. (p. 178)

5. (c) People who display the authoritarian personality display exaggerated submission to authority, extreme levels of conformity to conventional standards of behavior, self-righteous hostility, and punitiveness toward deviants and members of minority groups. (p. 178)

6. (d) Benevolent paternalism occurs when members of two groups may have close and affectionate relationships with each other, as long as the subordinates "stay in their place." (pp. 179-180)

7. (b) According to the typicality effect, people's attitudes and behaviors are most likely to be guided by their group stereotypes when the target of those attitudes and behaviors conforms to the particular group stereotype. (p. 183)

8. (c) Ambiguous or inadequate information about an individual member of an outgroup is especially likely to lead people to rely on stereotypes. Stereotypes are also more likely to be applied in the face of reports that an individual committed a single contrary act than if there was information that the stereotype-inconsistent information has been typical of the person. (pp. 183-184)

9. (a) Subtyping is the process of making finer distinctions within large group categories, and is a way of preventing stereotype change because it helps to explain disconfirming evidence (p. 184)

10. (b) Merely being arbitrarily categorized into groups induced students to show more favorable attitudes toward members of the in-group than the out-group. This was shown through Tajfel's minimal intergroup situation. (pp. 186-187)

11. (c) Group-serving biases are a clear example of ingroup favoritism. People tend to make more sympathetic attributions for an ingroup's successes and failures than for the outgroup's outcomes. (p. 187)

12. (c) The outgroup homogeneity effect refers to people's tendency to see the outgroup as more homogeneous than the ingroup in terms of traits, personality, and even number of subtypes. (p. 187)

13. (c) Brewer's theory of optimal distinctiveness suggests that people have two competing needs: for inclusion in larger collectives and for differentiation from other people. (p. 188)

14. (c) The idea that a decline in old-fashioned racism is more apparent than real and that the only real change has been in people's increased unwillingness to admit prejudicial attitudes is illusory change. (p. 192)

15. (a) According to aversive racism, to maintain an unprejudiced self-image, whites may discriminate against blacks only when there is a plausible nonracism justification for their actions. (pp. 193-194)

16. (c) Implicit stereotypes involve automatic activation. (pp. 194-195)

17. (d) Gordon Allport's contact theory identified several specific conditions that might help contact reduce prejudice, including acquaintance potential, cooperative independence, and equal status contact. (p. 199)

18. (b) The jigsaw technique is a contact technique that has been found to increase peer liking across ethnic and racial groups, to increase the self-esteem of minority children, and to improve academic performance. (p. 200)

19. (b) Recategorization focuses on the cognitive bases of stereotyping as a means of reducing prejudice. (p. 201)

20. (d) The most extreme negative evaluations were of the double outgroup. (p. 201)

True-False

1.	T (p. 169)		6.	T (p. 189)
2.	T (p. 169)		7.	T (p. 191)
3.	F (p. 178)		8.	T (p. 193)
4.	T (p. 179)		9.	F (p. 198)
5.	T (p. 180)		10.	T (p. 201)

Fill-in-the-Blank

1. Stereotypes (p. 170)
2. stereotype threat (p. 172)
3. ethnocentrism (p. 173)
4. discrimination (p. 174)
5. reverse discrimination (p. 174)
6. displaced aggression (p. 178)
7. Legitimizing myths (p. 180)
8. egoistic deprivation/ fraternal deprivation (p. 180)
9. ingroup favoritism effect (p. 186)
10. assumed similarity effect (p. 187)

Chapter 7: Social Influence

Multiple Choice

1. (a) Conformity is the tendency to change one's beliefs or behaviors in ways that are consistent with group standards. (p. 205)

2. (c) College men with good eyesight and presumably sharp minds gave the wrong answer about 35% of the time. (p. 207)

3. (b) People living in individualistic cultures tend to emphasize the negative aspects of conformity. Group pressure to conform is seen as a threat to the uniqueness of the individual. (p. 208)

4. (b) Informational influence occurs when a person is uncertain of the correct response and so uses group behavior as a guide to action. This is illustrated in Sherif's study. (pp. 209-210)

5. (a) Conformity due to the desire for social approval is known as normative influence. (p. 210)

6. (d) When conformity is based on informational influence or the belief that others are right, people usually change their minds and their behaviors. (p. 210)

7. (b) Asch found that increasing the size of the group past four did not increase the amount of conformity in his line judgment task. (p. 211)

8. (d) Providing information showing that healthy behavior is, in fact, "normal" in an attempt to change others' attitudes and behaviors is an example of social norms marketing. (p. 212-213)

9. (c) Double minorities or people who differ from the majority in two ways are also called "out-group minorities." (p. 215)

10. (d) Referent power has special relevance to personal relationships and groups. (pp. 217-218)

11. (a) Environmental manipulations occur when an influencer changes the situation so that the target of influence must comply. (p. 218)

12. (c) The expectation in American culture that people should help those who are less fortunate and, therefore, it is legitimate for those in need to ask for help is the norm of social responsibility. (p. 218)

13. (c) Forgas found that people in a positive mood evaluated a request more favorably than people in a neutral or negative mood. (p. 219)

14. (a) Increasing compliance by inducing a person to agree first to a small request is the foot-in-the-door technique. (p. 220)

15. (b) Increasing compliance by first asking for a very large request and then making a smaller request is the door-in-the-face technique, and is closely related to bargaining. (p. 222)

16. (a) The compliance technique in which a person is asked to agree to something on the basis of incomplete information and is later told the full story is the low-ball technique. (pp. 222-223)

17. (d) Increasing someone's compliance with a request by making a unique request that disrupts his or her refusal script is an example of the pique technique. (p. 223)

18. (d) The basic idea in reactance theory is that people try to maintain their personal freedom of action. (p. 224)

19. (c) Sixty-five percent of the participants in the Milgram study proceeded to give the highest level of shock. (p. 227)

20. (b) Miller's suggestion that evil acts are not necessarily performed by abnormal or "crazy" people is called the normality thesis. (pp. 228-229)

True-False

1. F (p. 206)
2. T (p. 208)
3. T (p. 209)
4. T (p. 211)
5. T (p. 212)
6. F (p. 212)
7. F (p. 215)
8. T (p. 215)
9. F (p. 218)
10. F (p. 227)

Fill-in-the-Blank

1. the information that the group provides us (p. 209)
2. right/ liked (pp. 209-210)
3. Commitment (p. 211)
4. desire for individuation (p. 212)
5. the dual-process hypothesis (p. 215)
6. Compliance (p. 215)
7. coercion (p. 217)
8. information power (p. 217)
9. a legitimate authority (p. 218)
10. that's not all (p. 223)

Chapter 8: Interpersonal Attraction

Multiple Choice

1. (b) The absence of an intimate attachment figure might produce emotional loneliness. (p. 235)

2. (c) Results from the study by Williams et al. (2001) showed that participants in the ostracism condition clearly experienced a sense of exclusion from the group and showed a decrease in mood and self-esteem. (p. 236)

3. (b) Avoidant attachment occurs when the parent is generally unresponsive or even rejecting. (p. 237)

4. (c) Adults who seek intimacy but worry that others will not reciprocate their love and will not stay with them are called anxious/ambivalent. (p. 239)

5. (d) In the 1950s, Festinger and his colleagues studied the proximity effect in Westgate West, a large apartment complex. (pp. 240-241)

6. (b) Memorable interactions are recent instances in which people have discussed something of personal importance with another person. (p. 241)

7. (c) The mere exposure effect refers to increased liking as a result of frequent exposure to a person or object. Thus, people show a preference for the letters in their own name because they are frequently exposed to those letters. (p. 242)

8. (d) Three plausible mechanisms have been proposed to explain why people in close relationships have similar attitudes: selective attraction, social influence, and environmental factors. (p. 246)

9. (c) For many years, laws banning interracial marriages were the norm in the United States. In 1967, the U.S. Supreme Court struck down the last of these state laws. (p. 246)

10. (c) About 30% of the breakups described by students involved a fatal attraction of one kind or another. (p. 249)

11. (b) People often find that it is rewarding to be seen with a particularly attractive person because they think it will enhance their public image, a phenomenon referred to as the radiating effect of beauty. (p. 251)

12. (c) Psychological research suggests that the Internet is neither inherently good nor inherently bad. (pp. 252-253)

13. (a) Studies of college students have found that a partner's physical attractiveness was considered a necessity by men but a luxury by women. (p. 253)

14. (c) Two contrasting explanations have been offered to explain the consistent sex differences in mate selection. A sociocultural perspective emphasizes that men and women have traditionally had distinct social roles. Evolutionary theorists have proposed that men and women have evolved different mating preferences to maximize their reproductive success. (p. 254)

15. (d) Buss proposed the evolutionary theory that men and women have evolved different mating preferences to maximize their reproductive potential. (p. 254)

16. (c) The practical or pragmatic lover seeks contentment rather than excitement. (p. 257)

17. (c) Attachment is not a component of Sternberg's triangular theory of love, which is characterized by intimacy, passion, and commitment. (pp. 259-260)

18. (d) According to Sternberg, infatuated love is the experience of passion without intimacy or commitment, as in "puppy love." (p. 260)

19. (a) According to Sternberg, liking is the experience of intimacy without passion or commitment. (p. 260)

20. (a) The relationship between dependency and jealousy is positive. A person who is highly dependent is more susceptible to jealousy. (p. 261)

True-False

1. F (p. 237)
2. T (p. 237)
3. T (pp. 237-238)
4. T (p. 239)
5. T (p. 248)
6. T (p. 249)
7. F (p. 250)
8. T (p. 256)
9. T (p. 257)
10. F (p. 259)

Fill-in-the-Blank

1. secure (p. 237)
2. working model (p. 238)
3. social exchange theory (p. 240)
4. proximity (pp. 240-241)
5. mere-exposure effect (p. 242)
6. phantom-other (pp. 244-245)
7. fatal flaws (p. 249)
8. trust and self-disclosure (p. 257)
9. love styles (p. 257)
10. Companionate love (p. 259)

Chapter 9: Close Relationships

Multiple Choice

1. (b) According to your text, the most influential perspective on social interaction is provided by interdependence theory. (p. 265)

2. (c) In terms of interdependence theory, costs are the negative consequences that occur in an interaction or relationship. An interaction might be costly because it requires a great deal of time and energy, because it entails much conflict, or because other people disapprove of the relationship and criticize us for being involved in it. (p. 266)

3. (b) Foa and Foa distinguished classified rewards along two dimensions: particularism and concreteness. Concreteness captures the distinction between tangible rewards and nonconcrete or symbolic rewards. (p. 266)

4. (a) The quality of outcomes a person believes he or she deserves is reflected in the comparison level. (p. 267)

5. (b) People in a relationship who share common interests and goals are said to have correspondent outcomes. (p. 267)

6. (c) Social roles are clusters of rules about how people should behave in a particular type of interaction or relationship. (p. 268)

7. (b) Equity and distributive justice are two names for the same thing. (p. 269)

8. (d) Equity theory has four basic assumptions. In addition to the three listed here is a fourth: Individuals who perceive inequity in a relationship will take steps to restore equity. (p. 269)

9. (d) People can attempt to restore equity in a relationship in two ways. One approach is to restore actual equity. A second approach is to use cognitive strategies to alter the perception of the imbalance, thus restoring psychological equity. (pp. 269-270)

10. (d) Mills and Clark have distinguished between exchange and communal relationships. These two types of relationships can be distinguished along all of the dimensions listed here. (p. 271)

11. (b) Evaluative disclosures occur when we reveal our personal opinions and feelings – our affection for another person, our guilt about being overweight, or how much we hate our current job. (p. 272)

12. (b) People may reveal or conceal information as a means of social control. For instance, people may deliberately refrain from talking about themselves in order to protect their privacy. (pp. 272, 274)

13. (a) Liking and self-disclosure are positively related. We are more likely to disclose to those we like, and we tend to like those to whom we disclose. (p. 273)

14. (d) Among Derlega's risks of self-disclosure are indifference, rejection, loss of control, and betrayal. (p. 274)

15. (d) For U.S. couples, higher satisfaction was associated with greater verbal disclosure. The same was also true of Indian women in love-based marriages. (p. 275)

16. (d) Research on African-American, Latino, and Caucasian marriages demonstrate few overall differences in the frequency of egalitarian, male-dominant, and female-dominant relationships. (pp. 280-281)

17. (b) A resource is anything that can be used to satisfy or frustrate needs or move people from or closer to their goals. (p. 281)

18. (a) Conflicts that focus on a partner's motives or personality fall into the personal dispositions category. (p. 283)

19. (c) Constraint commitment is based on negative forces or barriers that make it costly for a person to leave a relationship. Two important types of constraints are the lack of attractive alternatives and investments we have already made in the relationship. (p. 286)

20. (c) From the perspective of continuing the relationship, loyalty and voice are constructive, relationship-promoting responses; neglect and exit are destructive to the relationship. (p. 294)

True-False

1.	F (p. 266)	6.	T (p. 271)
2.	T (p. 266)	7.	T (p. 274)
3.	T (p. 266)	8.	T (p. 276)
4.	T (p. 267)	9.	T (p. 285)
5.	F (p. 270)	10.	T (p. 294)

Fill-in-the-Blank

1. Interdependence theory (p. 263)
2. comparison level for alternatives (p. 267)
3. equality (p. 269)
4. Equity (p. 269)
5. communal (p. 271)
6. Self-clarification (p. 272)
7. women /men /men (p. 276)
8. Intimacy (p. 277)
9. Social power (p. 279)
10. avoidance (p. 292)

Chapter 10: Behavior in Groups

Multiple Choice

1. (a) Zajonc distinguished between dominant and nondominant tasks. A nondominant task is one that is not well-learned, such as learning to drive a stick-shift car, and is interfered with by the presence of others. (p. 298)

2. (b) The idea that the presence of other people can motivate us because we are concerned about how those others will evaluate us is evaluation apprehension. (p. 299)

3. (b) According to the biopsychological approach, when the individual's resources are insufficient to meet the demands of the task, a threat response occurs. (p. 300)

4. (d) Max Ringelmann conducted the initial research on social loafing in the late 1880s. (p. 300)

5. (c) Karau and Williams (1993) proposed an integrative framework for understanding social loafing. According to their model, how hard an individual works on a group task depends on the person's belief about how important or necessary his or her own contribution is to group success and how much the person values the potential outcome of group success. (p. 301)

6. (a) Social compensation refers to the phenomenon by which people will sometimes work harder when in a collective setting to compensate for others in the group. (p. 302)

7. (d) LeBon (1896) used the term social contagion to refer to the infectious nature of mob behavior. (p. 305)

8. (b) Several theories of crowding have been proposed, including sensory overload, loss of control, and attributions. (p. 307)

9. (d) People in a group develop patterns of behavior, divide tasks, and adopt different roles. These patterns are referred to as the group structure. (p. 309)

10. (c) Diffuse status characteristics are general attributes of a person, such as age, sex, ethnicity, or wealth, that people tend to associate with ability. This concept is part of the expectation states theory. (p. 310)

11. (a) An additive task is one in which group productivity is the sum of the effort of each group member. Group productivity is generally superior to the efforts of any one person. (pp. 311-312)

12. (b) In an additive task situation, social loafing may diminish each individual's contribution, so that the group product is less than the anticipated sum of the individual inputs. (pp. 311-312)

13. (b) With conjunctive tasks, group productivity is only as good as the least competent group member or the "weakest link." (p. 312)

14. (b) "Freewheeling suggestions are discouraged" is not a rule of brainstorming. Rather, in brainstorming, freewheeling suggestions are encouraged. (p. 313)

15. (d) Social matching refers to the fact that most members of a brainstorming group tend to perform at relatively similar levels. (p. 314)

16. (a) When the topic is familiar, the alternatives are limited, and there is no correct answer, a majority-wins rule often prevails. (pp. 314-315)

17. (a) The idea that discussion causes individuals to focus on their group membership is the social identity process. This process leads individuals to feel pressure to shift their own views to conform with the perceived norm of the group. (p. 318)

18. (c) "The group encourages disagreeing opinions" is not a characteristic of groupthink. Rather, group members are discouraged from expressing disagreement. (p. 318)

19. (d) In a typical trial, both sides would try to use the road and would meet in the middle, head on. They would stubbornly stay there for awhile, each refusing to retreat. The players might laugh nervously or make nasty comments. Finally one of them would back up, erect the barrier, and use the alternative route. On the next trial they would do the same thing, and so it went. An occasional cooperative trial might occur, but most trials were competitive. (pp. 320-321)

20. (c) One of the findings from a recent meta-analysis of 45 studies stated that women scored higher than men on measures of transactional leadership. (p. 331)

True-False

1. F (p. 298)
2. T (p. 298)
3. F (p. 301)
4. T (p. 303)
5. T (pp. 305-306)
6. F (p. 306)
7. T (p. 317)
8. T (p. 317)
9. T (p. 318)
10. T (p. 325)

Fill-in-the-Blank

1. social loafing (pp. 300-301)
2. Social impact theory (p. 303)
3. Deindividuation (p. 305)
4. social density (p. 306)
5. cohesiveness (p. 311)
6. the common knowledge effect (p. 316)
7. cooperative (p. 323)
8. social dilemma (pp. 325-326)
9. Task/social (p. 328)
10. contingency model of leadership effectiveness (p. 329)

Chapter 11: Gender

Multiple Choice

1. (b) Beliefs about the personal attributes of males and females are gender stereotypes. (p. 336)

2. (d) Archer created the term face-ism to refer to the tendency for the media to emphasize men's faces and women's bodies. (p. 337)

3. (b) Personal stereotypes are our own unique beliefs about the attributes of groups of people, such as women and men. (p. 338)

4. (c) John Williams and Deborah Best studied gender stereotypes among college students in 25 countries around the world. They found that the core elements of gender stereotypes are quite similar across countries. (pp. 338-339)

5. (d) One way in which we can think about the sexes is in terms of subtypes of males and females. For example, mothers, career women, and beauty queens are subtypes of women. (p. 339)

6. (c) The activation of stereotypes is determined by both the amount of information available about a person and the salience of the person's group membership. Power also influences stereotype activation. (pp. 341-342)

7. (a) Paying attention enables subordinates to form more complex and usually less stereotypical impressions of their bosses. The powerful don't need to pay careful attention because they are in control, and therefore more likely to form stereotyped impressions of their subordinates. (p. 342)

8. (b) People sometimes act in ways that turn stereotypes into self-fulfilling prophecies. They behave toward people in ways that elicit stereotype-confirming behavior. (p. 344)

9. (c) Women tend to receive more negative ratings than men when they adopt a task oriented and directive leadership style, when they work in a traditionally masculine job, and when they are evaluated by men. (p. 346)

10. (b) There is some evidence that men's success is more likely to be attributed to ability, whereas women's success is more likely to be attributed to effort. (p. 347)

11. (a) Gender identity is usually acquired by age 2 or 3. (p. 347)

12. (c) People describing themselves as transgendered challenge the traditional view that gender is a simple male-versus-female dichotomy. (p. 349)

13. (d) A person who is low on both masculinity and femininity is undifferentiated. (p. 350)

14. (a) The congruence model proposes that adjustment is enhanced when there is an "appropriate" match between gender and self-concept. (p. 350)

15. (d) Self-ratings of traits such as emotional, kind, and helpful to others are called measures of communion or expressivity. (p. 352)

16. (b) Negative agency is also called unmitigated agency and has been conceptualized as a tendency to focus on the self to the exclusion of others and to go beyond assertion to hostility toward others. (p. 352)

17. (b) According to the socialization perspective, the many different social experiences of boys and girls lead to relatively enduring sex differences in attitudes, interests, skills, and personalities that continue into adulthood. (p. 354)

18. (d) Eagly found 62 studies of sex differences in persuasion, and only 16% found women were more easily persuaded. She also found 61 studies of responses to group pressures for conformity, and 34% found that women conformed significantly more than men. (p. 359)

19. (d) Researchers are not certain about the reason for this sex difference, but possible explanations include genetics, expectations and training, and a relationship-oriented outlook on life. (p. 360)

20. (d) Today, the majority of married women have paying jobs. (p. 366)

True-False

1.	F (pp. 335-336)	6.	T (p. 347)
2.	T (p. 338)	7.	T (p. 352)
3.	T (p. 341)	8.	T (p. 353)
4.	T (p. 342)	9.	F (p. 363)
5.	F (p. 342)	10.	F (p. 365)

Fill-in-the-Blank

1.	gender typing (p. 335)	6.	gender self-concept (p. 349)
2.	cultural (p. 338)	7.	androgynous (p. 349)
3.	gender subtypes (p. 339)	8.	meta-analysis (p. 357)
4.	gender identity (p. 347)	9.	men/women/physical aggression/ verbal aggression (p. 358)
5.	transsexual (p. 348)	10.	personal entitlement (p. 362)

Chapter 12: Helping Behavior

Multiple Choice

1. (c) Prosocial behavior is a much broader category than altruism. It includes any act that helps or is designed to help others, regardless of the helper's motives. (p. 373)

2. (d) According to Robert Trivers (1971), natural selection may have favored a disposition to feel guilt and a tendency to enforce mutual helping through social means such as punishment of those who don't follow group rules. This view emphasizes the biological basis of reciprocal altruism, which also explains the evolutionary approach to altruism. (p. 375)

3. (d) The norm of social justice refers to rules about fairness and the just distribution of resources. (p. 376)

4. (d) According to the sociocultural perspective of helping, people learn about the rules and guidelines for prosocial behavior through the process of socialization. (p. 377)

5. (d) Children will share their toys and candy more when they have been rewarded for sharing. (p. 378)

6. (a) Wanda was offering dispositional praise because she was emphasizing Susan's personality. (p. 379)

7. (c) Observational learning is best associated with modeling. They are two names for the same thing. (p. 379)

8. (a) The first step in the decision-making perspective of helping is perceiving a need. Someone must notice that something is happening and that help is required. (p. 380)

9. (d) According to Shotland and Huston (1979), there are five characteristics that lead people to perceive an event as an emergency: something happens suddenly and unexpectedly, there is a clear threat of harm to a victim, the harm to the victim is likely to increase over time unless someone intervenes, the victim is helpless and needs outside assistance, and some sort of effective intervention is possible. (p. 381)

10. (a) Attributing a person's plight to uncontrollable causes may elicit sympathy. (p. 384)

11. (c) The concept that best explains Brittany's willingness to help is the mood maintenance hypothesis. She may be helping to prolong her positive emotional state. (pp. 384-385)

12. (a) The negative-state relief model suggests that people in a bad mood may help to relieve their own discomfort. (p. 385)

13. (b) A person who is high in empathy has feelings of sympathy and concern for a person in need. People motivated by empathic concern usually intervene to help a person in need. (p. 386)

14. (b) Men are especially likely to help when the victim or requester is female, and when there is an audience. Men are also more likely to help strangers in distress than women. (p. 390)

15. (a) When others are present, people typically feel that someone else will intervene in an emergency, reducing their own feelings of personal responsibility. This is referred to as the bystander effect. (p. 392)

16. (c) A decision-making analysis of helping offers several suggestions as to why the presence of others inhibits helpfulness. Among these are the diffusion of responsibility, the ambiguity in the interpretation of the situation, and evaluation apprehension. (pp. 392-393)

17. (d) Research has identified several functions that volunteering can serve. Among these is self-enhancement, the idea that volunteering provides opportunities for personal growth and enhanced self-esteem. (p. 397)

18. (b) According to attribution theory, people are motivated to understand why they need help and why others are offering to help them. (p. 399)

19. (a) Reactance theory offers insights into the experience of receiving help. Older adults receiving aid from a spouse frequently reported feeling dependent, weak, or incapable. (p. 400)

20. (b) Men are more likely than women to have problems with drug and alcohol abuse, but they are less likely than women to seek help for these problems. (p. 401)

True-False

1.	F (p. 373)	6.	T (p. 384)
2.	T (p. 375)	7.	T (p. 387)
3.	T (p. 378)	8.	F (p. 392)
4.	T (p. 382)	9.	F (pp. 396-397)
5.	T (p. 384)	10.	F (p. 399)

Fill-in-the-Blank

1. altruism (p. 373)
2. social responsibility (p. 374)
3. social justice (p. 375)
4. learning perspective (pp. 379-380)
5. personal responsibility (p. 382)
6. uncontrollable/controllable (p. 384)
7. positive moods/negative moods (p. 385)
8. negative-state relief model (p. 385)
9. empathy/personal distress (p. 386)
10. bystander intervention (p. 391)

Chapter 13: Aggression

Multiple Choice

1. (c) Sociobiologists argue that all aspects of social behavior, including aggression, can be understood in terms of evolution. (p. 406)

2. (b) Prosocial acts of aggression are dictated by social norms. (p. 407)

3. (d) Sanctioned aggression refers to acts of aggression that fall somewhere between prosocial and antisocial. These acts are not required by social norms but are well within their bounds. An example is a coach disciplining a disobedient player. (p. 407)

4. (c) The well-established relationship between hot temperatures and violence may reflect frustration. The irritation and discomfort that accompany hot temperatures may be misattributed to interpersonal tension, which may produce aggression. (p. 408)

5. (b) The original frustration/aggression hypothesis suggested that aggression always follows from frustration and frustration always leads to aggression. (p. 408)

6. (c) A main mechanism that determines human aggressive behavior is past learning. (p. 409)

7. (b) The Bobo doll experiment by Bandura and his colleagues illustrated imitative learning of aggressive behavior. (p. 410)

8. (b) Parents are both the major source of reinforcement and the chief object of imitation for children. (p. 410)

9. (a) Historically, the southern United States has led the rest of the nation in homicide rates, in part because of the southern culture of honor. (p. 414)

10. (b) Competition over limited or scarce resources (e.g., countries competing for specific territories) reflects realistic group conflict. (pp. 416-417)

11. (b) A number of factors can produce deindividuation, including anonymity. All of the other factors listed here would likely decrease the likelihood of deindividuation. (p. 417)

12. (d) Contagious violence, mob behavior, and deindividuation are all examples of imitative aggression. (p. 417)

13. (d) Aggression anxiety has been found to be higher among women, children from middle-income as opposed to lower-income households, and children whose parents used reasoning and withdrawal of affection as disciplinary techniques. (p. 419)

14. (d) Marijuana has been shown in experimental studies to reduce aggression. (p. 421)

15. (c) In general, displaced aggression is most likely to be directed toward targets who are perceived as weaker and less dangerous. (p. 422)

16. (d) Most of the perpetrators of school violence have been young white males. Most have a history of social problems, although not necessarily ones relating to aggression. In some cases, a pattern of being bullied or taunted or feeling like an outsider have been implicated. (p. 423)

17. (b) The generalizability of laboratory research to the real world is external validity. (p. 426)

18. (d) Recent analysis of television programs indicate that TV violence in fact impairs memory both for brands and for the content of advertisements. (p. 427)

19. (a) One solution to the problem of demand characteristics is to collect the dependent variable under different auspices and in a wholly different context from the films, thus disguising the connection between the two. This is called a "separated posttest." (p. 430)

20. (b) Half of male college students reported that they had forced sexual activity on a woman, but only 15 percent said they would rape a woman if they could get away with it. The men did not seem to realize that there is no difference between rape and forcing a woman to have sex against her will. (p. 434)

True-False

1. T (p. 405)
2. F (p. 408)
3. T (p. 411)
4. T (p. 417)
5. F (pp. 417-418)
6. F (p. 419)
7. T (p. 422)
8. T (pp. 424-425)
9. F (p. 432)
10. T (p. 435)

Fill-in-the-Blank

1. Anger (p. 407)
2. sanctioned aggression (p. 407)
3. instrumental aggression (p. 416)
4. Deindividuation/dehumanization (p. 417)
5. disinhibiting effects (p. 420)
6. Catharsis (p. 422)
7. members of the public/ employees (p. 423)
8. correlational (p. 426)
9. desensitization (p. 430)
10. sexual harassment (pp. 436-437)

Chapter 14: Social Psychology and Health

Multiple Choice

1. (c) According to the "In the News" section, fifty percent of the U.S. population is now overweight or obese. (p. 440)

2. (d) The psychological study of health considers four main areas. In addition to the three listed, a fourth is identifying the causes and correlates of health and of illness and other dysfunctions. (p. 441)

3. (a) The practice of health behaviors centers on five sets of beliefs: general health values, perception of a health threat, personal vulnerability, self-efficacy, and response efficacy. Subjective norms is not one of these beliefs; rather, it is a component of the theory of reasoned action. (p. 444)

4. (b) Self-efficacy is the belief that one can perform a particular behavior that will be effective in reducing a health threat. (p. 445)

5. (a) Because her aunt recently died of smoking-induced lung cancer, the threat of lung cancer is personally relevant to Patricia. Generally speaking, when a health threat is perceived to be personally relevant, it is more likely to be processed systematically through central attitude-change routes. (p. 447)

6. (a) When people have an opportunity to affirm important values, their self-image becomes more positive, and therefore, paradoxically, these good feelings about the self enable them to confront personally relevant, potentially threatening information. (p. 448)

7. (d) Several factors contribute to making events be perceived as stressful. Among these variables are unpleasant or negative events, uncontrollable or unpredictable events, ambiguous events, and unresolvable issues. (p. 450)

8. (b) The relationship between prolonged stress and prosocial behavior is inverse. (p. 450)

9. (b) Interpersonal conflicts are by far the most distressing daily hassles. (p. 452)

10. (d) These are examples of emotion-focused coping methods because they involve efforts to regulate emotional reactions to stressful events. (p. 452)

11. (c) Active coping methods include seeking information, planning, and attempting to get help from others. Acceptance is an emotion-focused coping method. (p. 453)

12. (d) For women in the United States, acceptance predicted better pregnancy outcomes, whereas for Japanese women social assurance predicted a better outcome. (p. 454)

13. (d) Coping efforts are generally considered to be more successful if they reduce physiological arousal, if the person returns quickly to his or her previous life activities, and if they reduce psychological distress. (p. 454)

14. (b) Personality problems such as neuroticism lead people to appraise events as more stressful, to become more distressed by problems, and to react more strongly to them. (p. 456)

15. (d) Social support can be provided in any of a number of different ways, including emotional concern, the provision of information, and instrumental aid. (p. 457)

16. (c) Social support may be most effective when it is "invisible." When people are aware that other people are going out of their way to help them, they experience emotional costs which mute the effectiveness of the social support they receive. (p. 458)

17. (d) A number of variables influence the recognition and interpretation of symptoms. Included among these are situational factors, people's expectations, culture, mood, life satisfaction, and experience. (p. 460)

18. (d) Organized, cognitive pictures of one's symptoms that influence one's illness related activities are illness schemas. (p. 460)

19. (b) Acute illnesses are short in duration with no long-term consequences and are believed to be caused by specific viral or bacterial agents. (p. 460)

20. (a) Treatments that seem "medical," like taking a prescribed pill, have higher adherence rates than those that don't, like using an over-the-counter ointment. (p. 463)

True-False

1. F (p. 442)
2. T (p. 448)
3. F (p. 449)
4. F (p. 449)
5. T (p. 455)
6. T (p. 457)
7. F (p. 458)
8. F (p. 459)
9. F (p. 461)
10. T (p. 465)

Fill-in-the-Blank

1. Health behaviors (p. 442)
2. health protection programs (p. 442)
3. Health beliefs (p. 444)
4. low (p. 445)
5. daily hassles (pp. 451-452)
6. Coping (p. 452)
7. Dispositional optimism (p. 455)
8. Hardiness (p. 456)
9. emotional concern (p. 457)
10. Cyclic illness (p. 461)

Chapter 15: Social Psychology and the Law

Multiple Choice

1. (d) The interesting study by Brigham et al. revealed that the clerks correctly identified the confederates only 34% of the time. In other words, only 2 hours after interacting with the confederates, the clerks misidentified them more than 65% of the time. (p. 470)

2. (c) Your book discusses five estimator variables: viewing opportunity, stress and arousal, weapon focus, own-race bias, and retention interval. Lineup biases is a system variable. (p. 470)

3. (d) Estimator variables are variables that concern the eyewitness and/or the situation in which the event is witnessed. (p. 470)

4. (a) Acquisition is the process of perceiving and interpreting information. (p. 470)

5. (d) People who are exposed to stress or other negative emotions tend to have accurate memories of the event itself, but less accurate or complete memories of what happened before and after the event. (p. 471)

6. (b) The own-race bias is an example of the out-group homogeneity effect. People are able to distinguish between members of their own racial group but often have the experience that people in other racial groups "all look alike." (p. 471)

7. (c) Research suggests that cross-racial contact diminishes the own-race bias. (pp. 471-472)

8. (c) The source-monitoring theory suggests that people retain memories of both an original event and post-event information. The problem is that people frequently have problems with a process called "source monitoring" or identifying where they learned various pieces of information. As a result, people may mistakenly conclude that pieces of post-event information came from their observations of an event. (p. 473)

9. (d) Eyewitnesses make the most accurate identifications when they are presented with sequential lineups. (p. 475)

10. (d) To increase accuracy in eyewitnesses' testimony, open-ended questions should be asked, and officials should emphasize to witnesses that perpetrators may or may not be in the police lineup. (p. 477)

11. (b) Coerced compliant false confessions occur when people are pressured to admit guilt but privately continue to believe in their own innocence. (p. 477)

12. (d) Lie detector test, polygraph test, and control question test are three different names for the same thing. (p. 480)

13. (c) At the beginning of each trial, a process known as voir dire is held for the selection of jurors. During voir dire, judges and/or attorneys question potential jurors about opinions or biases that could adversely affect their ability to render a fair verdict. (p. 481)

14. (a) Peremptory challenges can be used to eliminate jurors for a number of reasons, including occupation and perceived personality traits. (p. 481)

15. (a) Individuals who support the death penalty are more likely to convict than individuals who oppose the death penalty. (p. 482)

16. (b) Susan is using the story model. According to the story model, jurors use the evidence presented in trials to create stories about the events in question. (p. 483)

17. (b) The story model asserts that jurors reach verdicts through actively interpreting and evaluating the evidence they are given. (p. 483)

18. (a) According to Steblay, et al. (1999), exposure to negative pretrial publicity about a criminal suspect increases the likelihood that jurors will convict the individual. Pretrial publicity also affects civil cases. (p. 484)

19. (a) Aversive racism theory asserts that most people in contemporary U.S. culture believe in equality but still have some negative beliefs and feelings about black individuals. (p. 486)

20. (b) Research suggests that evidence-driven juries discuss the trial more thoroughly and therefore make better judgments about the case. (p. 488)

True-False

1. T (p. 470)
2. F (p. 471)
3. F (p. 475)
4. F (p. 476)
5. T (p. 479)
6. F (p. 479)
7. F (p. 480)
8. T (p. 486)
9. F (p. 488)
10. T (p. 488)

Fill-in-the-Blank

1. System (p. 470)
2. retrieval (p. 470)
3. weapon focus effect (p. 471)
4. own-race bias (p. 471)
5. sequential (p. 475)
6. minimization (p. 478)
7. Voir dire (p. 481)
8. death qualification (p. 482)
9. character (p. 485)
10. framework (p. 489)